THE LAST MISSION
The Incredible Story of William Kollar

Nikos Ligidakis

Copyright © October 2002 by William M. Kollar
and Nikos Ligidakis

First Printing, January 2012
All rights reserved. Printed in the United States of America. No part of this book may be reproduced in any form or by any means without permission in writing from publisher.

ISBN# 978-0-9728118-1-1

Library of Congress Control Number: 82985249535

Published by
Inkwell Productions
3370 N. Hayden Rod., #123-276
Scottsdale, AZ 85251
Phone (480) 315-9636
Fax (480) 315-9641
Toll Free 888-324-2665
Email: info@inkwellproductions.com
Website: www.inkwellproductions.com

To my son Wade Kollar

Table of Contents

Forward
Prologue
Chapter 1   Familiar Skies 1
Chapter 2   Shot Down 5
Chapter 3   The Gates To Hell.. 17
Chapter 4   Enemy Territory 21
Chapter 5   German Fury.. 29
Chapter 6   Lost, Then And Now 39
Chapter 7   On The Run 47
Chapter 8   Pain, A Constant Companion...................... 61
Chapter 9   Lost In The Mountains 69
Chapter 10 Rings On My Cane 79
Chapter 11 Reflections... 89
Chapter 12 The Highest Mountain 97
Chapter 13 Death In The Valley.................................... 105
Chapter 14 In No Man's Land....................................... 115
Chapter 15 Confusing Times 127
Chapter 16 The Big Feast 137
Chapter 17 Rolling Rivers And Steep Hills................. 149
Chapter 18 Dance With Me... 157
Chapter 19 To The Land Of Deliverance.................... 163
Chapter 20 A Nation Of Wanderers............................. 167
Chapter 21 In Anticipation Of Freedom 175
Chapter 22 Lift-Off... 181
Chapter 23 Ghosts Of The Past..................................... 185
Chapter 24 Proud Moments.. 193
Chapter 25 A New Life 201
Chapter 26 The Heartbeat Of War 213
Chapter 27 The Aftermath Of Wars 217
Chapter 28 A Full Circle 221
Epilogue   Eternal Dilemma 226

Forward

This is a tribute to all unsung heroes who have engaged in the controversial entity called war.
Those whom I have met as I was writing this book,
Those whom I have never known,
To all those who have fought for our freedom.
The men and women who have come from the ranks of civil society to fight in the wars that others created.
Those to whom history refers with the anonymous and cruel word "troops, "
The soldiers in the infantry and those in the cavalry,
The men and women in the air and at sea.
Since I was a child I had many questions:
Why do we have wars?
Why do we create massacres?
Why are young people brought to these theaters of war to suffer, to die?
I was told that wars were about glory and about victory.
But all I saw was the tragedy and the loss.
I believe that human suffering surpasses glory and tragedy.
Wars demonstrate a chain of events that intertwine because of actions that we personally did not commit.
In wars, our individual destiny is determined by the simple

gesture of somebody else, by means of a mechanism that is alien to our wishes and our will.
My friend, look at those butchered in wars.
Any one of them could have been your son.
Our sons have been sent to the wars by those who have the privilege to hold the ultimate power, a power that is used capriciously to display absolute command, absolute power, a power that splits men's brains into a schizophrenic personality.
One side talks about democracy, peace and progress,
Yet the other side acts to destroy, to kill, to possess.
As long as humans create wars, the concept of killing in order to survive will remain unchanged and unchangeable;
Yesterday, today, tomorrow, forever.
I believe in man uniformed or not.
It is the structures, the systems, the powerful: it is those who turn man against m n,
It is those who disturb me.
I've always had the seductive urge to write books in which the story talks about human feelings,
That is why the story of William Kollar intrigues me.
William Kollar was one of those who survived the wars.
His incredible story takes on a freedom's run of hundreds of miles.
Miles full of danger, exhaustion, starvation, and death.
William Kollar is a fascinating character, one whom we are fortunate to know.

There are so many more whom we do not know.
There are those who we will never hear about, because they are on the stage for a short time,
Because they are dead,
They are the pilots and the gunners, the commandos, the sailors and the privates.
My friend, we are missing the point if we do not wonder who those soldiers are,
Those who fought to prove that life always wins.
Their names must be in the narrative of wars,
In the eternal story of man who in war manifests himself in all his truth, because nothing reveals as much as wars,
Nothing exacerbates with the same strength, beauty and ugliness.
Nothing else but war unmasks our courage and our cowardice.
Throughout the pages of this book you will meet an extra ordinary yet humble man, a man who has never forgotten those who paid the ultimate price of war.
Finally, I would like to say that it is difficult for me to comprehend what oratorical or psychological shrewdness persuades people to kill, to destroy, to devastate,
It makes me think that for some people reality and fantasy mean the same thing.
For those who oppose the killing and bombings, it has been a ferocious battle in order to stop the blood shed in favor of peace and equal co-existing.

It is a battle that will allow us to discover the inevitability of
destiny and provide us with the formula of life,
a formula which I have no reason to doubt exists.

— *Nikos Ligidakis*

WILLIAM KOLLAR
The Early Years in the Air Force

AG 201 Kollar, Wm. M. (Enl)   1st Ind.   RL/mp
HEADQUARTERS, MCTOUSA, Postal Division, APO 534, U. S. Army, 4 April, 1944.

TO: Commanding Officer, 415th Bomb Sq., 98th Bomb Gp.

    1. SGT. WILLIAM M. KOLLAR, 36175843 is shown to be a member of your command. Request that the letter be called to his attention and that reply be made direct to the writer who has not been informed to this reference.

By command of Lieutenant General DEVERS:

                                                ROY LEWIS,
                                                Major, A. G. D.,
                                                Ass't Adj. General.

                                  2nd Ind.   JKK/dar
415th Bomb Sq (H) AC, APO 520, Postmaster, New York, N.Y., 9, April 1944.

TO: Mrs. Dave Wondwyk, 206 Division St., Lowell, Michigan.

    1. Sgt. William Kollar was reported Missing in Action on April 2, 1944.

    For the Squadron Commander:

                                                J. KYLE KINDSOLVER,
                                                Captain, Air Corps,
                                                Adjutant.

Prologue

This is my story,

A story imprisoned within the compounds of my mind for twenty years.

A letter sent by mail freed this story from the restrictions of classified secrecy.

It was then that the faces, the sounds, and slowly the feelings began to come back.

Images of the war nested for long in my conscience were surfacing in my memory and growing in volume.

An urge to tell the story kept haunting me for years.

The story about a bomber crew shot down in enemy territory.

The crewmembers made a heroic run for freedom, a run that bonded us in life and death.

There were no records kept about this adventure, simply because we were not allowed to do so.

I estimated that our run for freedom covered several hundred miles.

We ran over the steep mountains of Yugoslavia, through the German-held valleys of a dangerous land divided into vicious guerilla warfare.

Bands of guerillas fought for their own causes; it was impossible to tell the enemy from a friend.

Our marathon ended thirty-four days after we were shot down over Steyr, Austria.

There were days of starvation, exhaustion, snow, sunshine and lice.

It was my last flying mission, where we lost thirty-seven planes and three hundred seventy men were left dead or missing in action.

When our plane was shot down, our bomber crew managed to land by parachute in Yugoslavia.

Some of us made it through despite impossible odds. Others did not.

There would have been many more thousands dead or missing in action if not for our pilots, those heroic men who brought back a myriad of wounded soldiers, flying their battle-damaged planes back to home base.

After we were shot down our crew was listed as MIA.

No one knew our fate as we made our way through a land of people who spoke a language that we could not understand.

Mayday for us came on Palm Sunday, April 2, 1944.

This is my story,

A story that recounts human tragedy and captures the triumph of the human spirit.

— William Kollar

WESTERN UNION

No 8 GD NB 43 Govt WUX Washington DC 2.4% PM 2/24/44

Mrs Pearl Woudwyke
206 Divn St
Lowell Mich

The Secretary of War desires me to express his deep regret that your son Staff Sargent William M Kollar has been reported missing in action since Two April over Austria. If further details or other information are rx received you will be promptly notifies

Dunlop Acting The Ajt General

Our Crew
From top left: Kollar, Jensen, Maloney, Waldo, Reilly, Fleming
Bottom from left: Birchfield, Brady*, Fetterman, Stryker

*Eddie Brady, pictured in white coat, our original pilot was shot down and captured by the Germans on a volunteer mission in Regensburg, Germany. He remained a POW until the end of the war.

CHAPTER 1

Familiar Skies

*P*olly and I sat on our front patio with our poodle, Jet, lying at my feet as usual. We watched water-skiers spraying plumes of water as they crisscrossed Lake Minnehaha. This had become an afternoon ritual as we waited for the mail to arrive. Jet let out a low growl, his way of letting us know the mail carrier had turned the corner a block away.

"Here comes the mail," Polly said. "Probably more bills."

"Good afternoon, Mr. and Mrs. Kollar," said the mailman as he approached our steps. Doug has delivered our mail for years, even Jet knows him as a friend when he approaches the house. Sorting through the mail, Polly handed me an official-looking letter.

"It's from the government. You're probably getting drafted," she said with a chuckle.

I opened the letter and read it carefully.

"What is it?" Polly asked, patiently waiting for my answer.

"Well," I said, "do you remember years ago, I told you that my escape from the Germans was a classified secret? The government has just released me from my secrecy obligation. Now I can tell my story."

I read the letter aloud to Polly, and was overcome with memories.

I wonder if Clarence got one of these? I should call him.

I should call everyone. Who is left?

As I read the letter, a strange calm washed over me.

When I finished it, I lay back in my chair and watched the long shadows dance in the breeze on the front lawn. Our American flag, flying from the front porch post, flapped back and forth. To the north, the orange groves were in full bloom, the foothills were painted with purple hues, crowned with scattered clouds, faintly amber. The sun on the far horizon was glowing brightly, pausing a moment before lighting up the sky with another glorious sunset. Gazing into this lazy Florida sky, I drifted off.

Suddenly I could hear the raucous roar of the bomber engines revving up for takeoff.

Fumes of gasoline and oil surrounded me. I felt the vibration of the aircraft as I was sitting in my chair. Faces of young men unfolded in my mind, young men who came from the ranks of a civil society, who were placed under intense pressure with the cruel choice of kill or be killed. Young men who, after a brief training were expected to be extraordinary and face the fury of the elite divisions of superbly trained Luftwaffe.

Every time we lifted off for a mission we wondered

if we'd survive.

Many young men did not. But, some of us did come back to our country with memories nested in our con sciences – memories that I had tried desperately to forget. Today's letter resurrected emotions of long ago.

My wife Polly sat by me. She has been my rock, my best friend. Even for her it is impossible to participate in my nostalgia for the most intense memories of my life.

It was from Lecce, Italy, that many of my friends began their last flight.

The airfield at Lecce, Italy

Clarence and Bill working on a B24 in our
Outfit – 98th Bomb Group

CHAPTER 2

Shot Down

*T*he military air base at Lecce, Italy, was veiled in damp and dark. It was Palm Sunday, April 2, 1944. In the pre-dawn chill, I walked around the B-24D that would take our crewmembers and me on yet another mission. Clarence, our flight engineer, was right behind me, double checking my pre-flight inspection.

"Maggie's Drawers" is what they call the flag that is thrown up on the firing range following a complete miss when you are shooting for qualification, and that was the name of our plane. On the nose of the plane was an outline of a pair of woman's underwear, the old fashioned kind with a full seat and lace around the leg holes. There were also small paintings of II drawers II for each of the plane's bombing m1ss1ons.

Our armament man, O'Conner, was checking the bombs and ammunition boxes. Reilly, our radioman, inspected and tested his electronic components. And Clark, our bombardier, was installing his Sperry bomb sight.

I stood in my gunman's position on the left side of the plane. The engines powered up, the aircraft vibrated furiously as it struggled to escape the runway and lift up over the city of Lecce. Maggie's Drawers lifted her nose from the runway and began to climb toward the heavens. We passed 1500 feet, the mark for oxygen use. I was grateful for the warmth of my heated suit and boots, and though my tight-fitting oxygen mask was uncomfortable, it protected my face from the cold air whipping through the plane.

We were on our way to Steyr, Austria, a five-hour trip one way. Our mission, known only to our pilot, Lt. Fred Stryker, and co-pilot, Lt. George Morell, Lt. Clark Fetterman, our bombardier, and William Birchfield, our navigator, was to drop a load of 500-pound bombs on the only ball bearing factory left to the Luftwaffe. It was an important target: the whole world of machinery runs on ball bearings. Without them it is impossible to manufactured or repair equipment.

A huge thundercloud had broken up overnight, and we brushed through scattered clouds as the plane lifted above 28,000 feet where the air is frigid and hostile.

We flew over the Adriatic Sea and into Yugoslavia. I was physically relaxed, yet a little apprehensive. This was my ninth mission and the second since I had spent three weeks in the hospital with malaria. I smiled grimly at the irony. I would rather be up here than lying in that dank, dark, cement hospital, overcome with chills and fever and wrapped in the excruciating pain of malarial cramps.

A few hours had passed since we left the base when the urgent message came over the intercom. "Enemy planes approaching at 3 o'clock."

The clear, loud voice in my earphones snapped me back to the present.

The 3 o'clock planes belonged to Joe Maloney, the gunner on the right side of the plane, and to the top and ball turret gunners. As soon as the planes were in range, all the gunners started firing.

A voice in the intercom yelled, "He's going down!" "More coming in at 9 o'clock," yelled another voice. The 9 o'clock planes were mine. There were three

Me-109s, approaching fast, like hawks in full dive; they came at us with guns blazing. I saw tracers racing out to meet them, fired by John Reilly, who manned the top gun turret, and a prickly sensation surfaced from beneath my skin. Twin 50s cut across the front of one Me-109, and as it came within my firing range, I fired several rounds at it. As soon as it left my firing range another one took its place.

I was hyped with a torrent of adrenaline, and images flooded my mind: Pearl Harbor and the American flag. The blood of freedom was awakened within me; so too was my courage.

Another plane came into my firing range and my 50 caliber gun answered its attack. The firing was fast and furious, and as it flew out of my range, yet another plane took its place. My machine gun chattered until the third plane, too, was out of range. My eyes scanned the sky for new targets.

The skies were clear for a brief moment, and it was

cold, cold, cold as the sub-zero wind screamed in our waist windows.

The seven planes of our formation held their position and their predetermined altitude as instructed. The Speery bombsights were very sensitive to any change of position, altitude or speed; any change would have made the bombs miss their target. I braced myself and concentrated on my gun sight and target. Hitting your target is a skillful act, as the German fighter planes would change position every few seconds, using evasive action to avoid our machine gun fire. The pilots of the planes, while fighting combat, never flew straight and level for more than a few seconds.

"Flak, 11 o'clock low," I heard the pilot say.

A stream of enemy tracer bullets, small glowing white-hot balls of fire, went whizzing past our aircraft. I knew some fragments must have struck the aircraft, but could see no damage from my position.

Our plane had several gun stations. William Birchfield was stationed at the nose turret with two 50-calibers; John Reilly was in the top turret with two more 50-calibers; Arthur Fleming sat in the tail turret with two more machine guns. O'Conner was in the fetal position in the ball turret at the bottom of the aircraft. Joe Maloney was on the right and I had the left waist gun position.

The sky was blackened with exploding anti-aircraft shells fired from the ground. The air raged with fire from our guns and those of the German planes. The German fighters flew through their own flak to get to us; the Me 1

09s were in and out like a flash. Some of them sustained battle damage from their own ground fire.

We were about ten minutes from our target when, out of the corner of my eye, I saw black smoke tracing the sky. It came from the back of our formation.

"Oh damn, it's Charlie!" I whispered to myself. Tail-End Charlie was the last plane of the formation. The tailing plane is always the most vulnerable to enemy fire.

Charlie swayed in the air like an acrobat on a tight rope who has lost his balance. I held my breath as the pilot fought for control, then I saw Charlie turn his nose down ward toward the ground; the plane disappeared from my sight, leaving behind an ugly scar of thick black smoke on the face of the sky.

I prayed for the boys of Charlie to escape and be safe, but I knew it was unlikely because the plane was spinning madly and was engulfed in flames.

The Germans had known all along that the ball bearing plant was our objective and they were defending it tenaciously. Several more fighters returned to attack our formation.

The battle was furious. Flak burst all around the formation. Heavy ammunition struck our ship. Our chances of survival were slim. We turned toward the target, and held our altitude and speed. Behind us I saw another B-24 from our formation go down. I could not tell which one it was; I was in an inferno of machine gun fire, anti-aircraft fire and smoke.

We were almost over the target. Ahead I could see meager sunlight reflected from a maze of red-tiled roofs. Through a slight haze, our pilot could see our target clearly. We reached it and dropped our full load of bombs onto two sizable buildings. As soon as the bombs were away, we banked left and started losing altitude so we could gain air speed and head for home.

There were five B-24 planes left in our formation. For a few moments, all was quiet, and then seven German fighters came at us again. One of them, an Me-109, flying just out of gun range. Suddenly, he lowered the nose of his aircraft and released several air rockets. These were the first air-to-air rockets we had seen in the war. I felt stripped of protection. There was nothing but paper-thin aluminum sheet metal between those powerful explosions and us.

More enemy fighters came from all angles; the sky was covered with enormous amounts of flak from the ground fire. The sky was filled with German planes. They were everywhere!

The tail and ball turrets reported that several two engine fighters were steadily firing into our formation. The German Me-109 was still glued to my wing. One of our P-47 fighters was following him, trying to shoot him down. The exchange of fire intensified. Flak exploded all around us. Then there was an abrupt jolt and explosion as one of the air to air rockets hit our plane. The rocket head went through our number three engine, knocking it out and at the same time putting number four engine out of commission. The rocket head was supposed to explode on impact; however, for some reason, it went through the wing and exploded some six yards after exiting the wing. Had it exploded on impact, the entire crew would have been killed.

The aircraft dropped sharply, and I struggled to keep my balance, my fingers still on the trigger of the machine gun. The right wing of Maggie's Drawers was badly damaged: engines three and four were out and the fuel lines to that wing were severed. A gas vapor trail appeared behind the wing, and it looked a mile long.

Maggie's Drawers was going down.

I worked to stay on my feet and shoot at the enemy fighters picking away at our disabled aircraft. I knew the pilot and the co-pilot had both feet on the left rudder, pushing with all their might, but the plane was still staggering like a drunken sailor.

Then the enemy fighters veered off; they had spotted another formation of B-24s about a mile off headed for the ball bearing plant. We saw them making passes at the formation, and then they were out of sight as our plane curved downward. At this point we pulled up the ball turret and got Sgt. O'Conner out and into the waist area where we all snapped our vest pack parachutes onto our harnesses.

I could hear the screech of the two remaining engines roaring at full power struggling to keep the B-24 aloft – and failing. Then the pilot's voice filled my ears. "We are losing altitude 500 feet per minute." His voice was calm. Fred was trying to get us as far away from the target as possible before bailing out. But every second was a risk; the plane was quickly filling up with high-octane fumes. One spark and it would explode into a ball of fire, killing everyone on board.

It is an amazing feeling as you stand between life and death, between the real and the surreal. Every power, every feeling that you possess surpasses the normal, to cope with a reality that has gone beyond what was thought before that moment to be impossible.

Suddenly the sound of bullets whined past our plane; a group of Me-109s had spotted us. They seemed to be on their way back to their base for refueling, but they took the time to make a few swipes at our limping aircraft. Somehow they missed vital areas and that appeared to aggravate them. A few broke from their formation to chase us.

We were sweating the possibility that just one spark could ignite the gasoline vapor trailing inside our plane and behind us, and we would be blown to pieces. We were approaching 8,000 feet when we spotted another formation of enemy planes headed our way. We were not one of their primary targets; they were simply taking some time to use us for target practice. They shot several holes in the fuselage. Miraculously, none of the members of our crew was seriously injured by their fire.

The pilot's voice came on again, "We are approaching

6,000 feet. The range of mountains ahead is 7,000 feet." The crash was inevitable.

The abandon ship bell rang out. "Mayday! Mayday! Bail Out!" I turned to the bottom escape hatch, but three men were already ahead of me. The seconds ticked away.

The mountains loomed closer.

I turned back to my gun position, prepared to jump from my waist window, but as soon as I put one foot out, enemy bullets ricocheted all around me. I hastily drew my foot back in. "What is wrong with them, shooting at people going down?" I was furious.

I grabbed my 50-caliber gun. Holding steady, I looked out. I couldn't believe what I saw: there, several yards away, were two fighters so close that they looked as if they were one enormous plane.

I imagined the pilots' faces behind their oxygen masks and I let my ammunition fly.

I knew instantly that I had hit the plane closest to me. I saw the burst of flames and the shrapnel scatter across the sky. As the first plane went down, the other fighter moved in closer through the fire and metal shards.

I knew the mountains were getting closer every moment.

I was trembling as I swung my gun toward the second fighter and fired away until the gun overheated and locked up. As soon as my heavy barrage hit him, black smoke began to pour from the plane. A moment later, the sky filled with debris and the defeated fighter's nose turned straight down into a death spiral engulfed in a ball of fire. A strange sensation overcame me; two forces collided inside of me, joy and sadness. Joy for the glory that welled up inside me, sadness for the lives lost. Those pilots had families to mourn them, too.

Turning quickly, I saw that the bottom escape hatch was clear, and as the plane tilted for its final descent into the mountainside, I jumped.

We were trained to count to ten before pulling the ripcord on our parachutes. I did not even count to one. I pulled the chord and the chute flew in my face, ripping my hat and goggles off. Flakes of mothballs flew into my nose, mouth and eyes, blinding and gagging me. I coughed and rubbed my eyes. I opened them just in time to witness Maggie's Drawers falling out of control, trailed by thick, black smoke. She vanished in a ball of fire on the side of the snow-capped mountain.

I saw several other chutes open in the air; I was trying to count to see if everyone had gotten out safely, when a German fighter appeared to my right. I stared, wide eyed, as he made a pass within a few feet of where I hung, helplessly, in the air currents. I braced myself for bullets or being run over. Then the German pilot waved at me and like a good fellow, I waved back. I didn't want any hard feelings at this point as he turned and made a second pass. The plane flew by so close it was almost touching my chute. Suddenly the plane turned away, g1vmg my chute the Me-109's prop wash. I wondered if the pilot had done that on purpose if his wave was a sarcastic "good-bye ti .

My chute stretched out straight and started to collapse. If the shroud lines tangled, it most likely would not open again.

My free fall began. I was falling fast without my parachute's support, buffeted by the wind whistling by my face.

I had just closed my eyes in despair when I felt myself abruptly being pulled upward – my eyes flew open and I was looking up into the graceful folds of my wide open parachute – the sun showing through its canopy spread out to hold me up. I began to breathe again.

As I hung in the air a visitor came by, a black bird. He circled me, checking me out. I smiled at my black flying friend. The sounds of engines roared above my head. Gunfire chattered on the horizon. I could not tell what direction it was coming from. The black bird swung around again, eyeing me with his head cocked to the side. I hung waiting for the ground to come up and meet me.

The black bird flew away, abandoning me as I fell into a strange land.

Shot Down

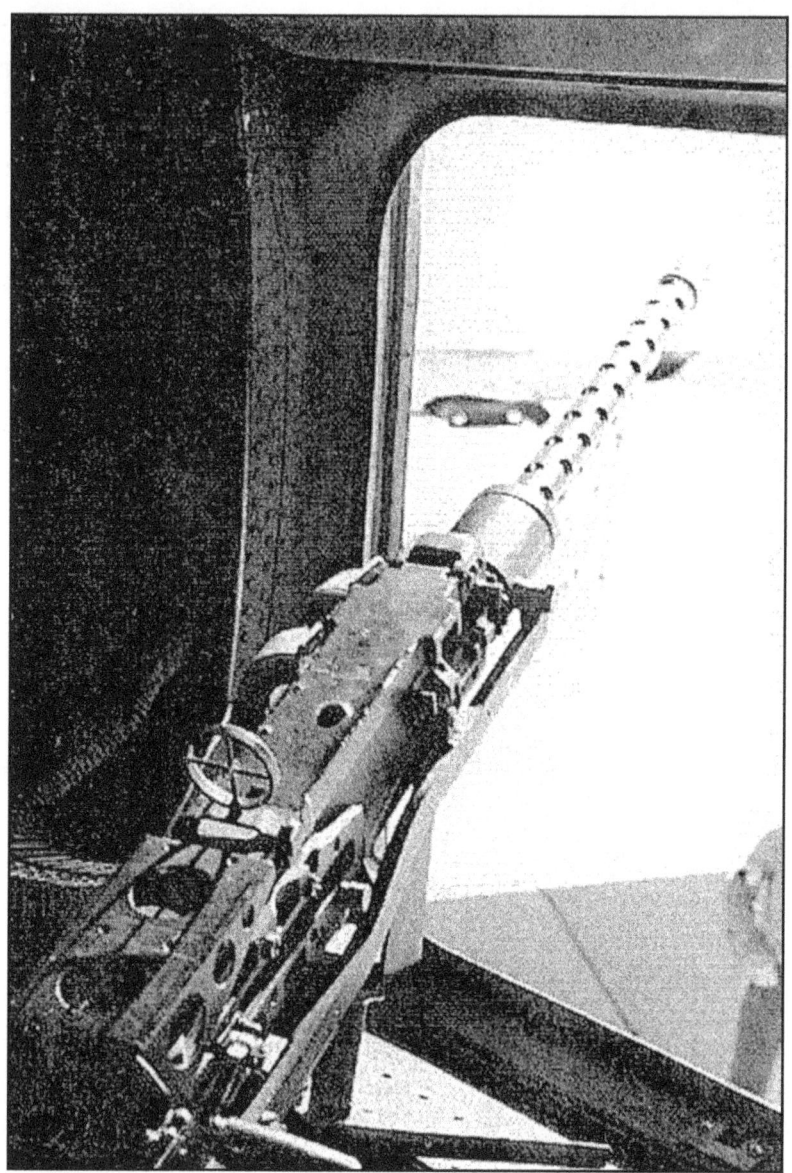

Waist window of a B24

CHAPTER 3

The Gates to Hell

As I fell, surrendering my fate to the unknown world below, a memory flashed in my mind. "We interrupt this program to bring you a special news bulletin. The Japanese have attacked Pearl Harbor!"

I remember that day well. I was sitting in Pete's Cafe, my favorite local diner in Lowell, Michigan, with a friend of mine, when the music coming from the radio was interrupted for this special announcement.

It was Sunday, December 7, 1941. I was off work while my leg healed from a bad burn that I got working on the construction of a new bridge. I had been pouring the hot tar between the new brick approaches. I transported the hot tar from the holding tank to the brick area using cans. On the day of the accident, as I carried a can full of boiling hot tar, I stepped off the curb and lost my balance. Just then the handle of the can broke loose, sending hot tar down my right leg. It clung to my flesh, causing a very deep third degree burn covering a 4 by 5 inch area of my right calf. The following weeks of recovery were extremely painful.

The Sunday morning that I heard the news about

the day which would go down in infamy, my leg was still heal mg.

The following morning, December 8, my four closest. friends and I hopped into the car and drove to the nearby recruiting office in Grand Rapids to sign up to serve our country.

My four friends were given reporting dates. I was told to come back after my leg had healed.

Meanwhile details of the attack were being reported: The first attack came at 7:53 a.m., when most of the crew-members were eating breakfast. The quiet of the morning was shattered by machine gun fire followed quickly by the sound of explosions. Within minutes, anti-aircraft guns returned the enemy fire. A bomb crashed through the two armored decks of the battleship Arizona, igniting its magazine. The explosion ripped the sides open. Within minutes the ship sank, taking 1,300 lives with her. That was just the first attack. The second wave of enemy planes came at 8:55 a.m. By 10 a.m., it was all over.

Approximately 460 enemy airplanes had attacked Pearl Harbor. They destroyed 118 U.S. planes, crippled or destroyed 18 battleships, and left 2,403 seamen dead and 1,178 wounded.

I went back to the recruiting office several times over the next few weeks, as I impatiently waited for my leg to mend.

In the meantime the United States and Britain declared war on Japan and the Japanese promptly declared war on the United States and Britain.

A few days later, Germany and Italy declared war on the United States, although Hitler had previously sought to avoid such a war with America while he pursued the battle with Russia.

Finally, I was given a report date: March 23, 1942. On that day, I reported to Battle Creek for induction, and from there I went to Missouri for basic training. As I entered the gate to Jefferson Barracks, I did not imagine that this gate would take me on the adventure of a lifetime – that this gate would take me to Hell on earth.

I was 22 years old.

Bill, standing by a damaged aircraft

Bill with Corporals Bill Dyer and Joe Paknik

CHAPTER 4

Enemy Territory

With squinting eyes, through dust and thin sun light reflecting off the snow, I saw below me sandcastles, dollhouses, and scurrying ants; as I floated downward they resolved into mountains, buildings, and people.

A group of men on foot and some riding motorcycles were sprinting in my direction from the village to the south. Another group of people came running from a canyon to the north. I could not tell if they were enemies or friends. I assumed they were all enemies. I prayed for a quicker descent. I planned to run east, parallel to the mountains, as soon as my feet hit the ground. I had to get out from between and away from the two groups running toward me.

I landed hard on a snowy slope, sliding down about 50 feet on my backside to the bottom of a small hill. My mind was preoccupied with escape, and I felt no pain. I stood up and hurriedly unfastened my chute. I looked around at an unfamiliar landscape and suddenly felt as though I had fallen back in time to a place before man's coming, an age-old land of danger and death.

Yelling to the south drew my attention. I looked and

saw Germans about a quarter of a mile away. I turned to run east but too late. A man was standing at the top of the small hill that I had slid down. He was pointing a machine gun at me.

"Ruskie!" he yelled in a commanding voice, his gun leveled at my chest. I sucked in a huge gulp of air and put out my hands in front of me.

"No! No! Americana!" I cried. He did not lower his gun.

I waited, hoping that he was an American sympathizer.

I knew that there were Yugoslavian guerillas fighting with the Allies, but there were also guerillas fighting for the Germans. A woman and three more men appeared at the top of the slope.

The first guerilla ran and slid down the bank. He was a big man, about 6 feet tall, unshaven, with clothes soiled from long travel. Suddenly, I noticed his left sleeve was empty – his arm gone. I braced myself as he ran down. He slung his gun across my back, hugged and kissed me on both cheeks. I sighed in relief.

The rest of the guerillas ran down the slope. Quickly they picked up my chute and ran back up into the canyon. They motioned for me to follow. I handed my 45-caliber handgun to the leader, as we had been instructed to do at headquarters if we met friendly forces. In training, we were told that if the Germans caught an armed airman, he could be shot as a spy.

He ran and I followed.

The canyon was narrow and long and strewn with rocks and boulders; there we met another small group of guerillas – more men and a woman appeared from behind the rocks ahead of us. We ran down the narrow gorge, between and over rocks, tramping through the snow, always looking behind and above us. Suddenly, against the band of blue sky above us we spied silhouettes, and machine gun fire rained down on us. The guerillas jumped to the sides of the canyons, took cover behind rocks, and returned fire. "Machine Gun" as I had taken to calling the one-armed man, grabbed me, pointed to a hole between the rocks, and motioned for me to crawl into it.

The Germans had abandoned the rim and entered the canyon. They were moving up behind us, going from rock to rock, moving steadily toward our hidden band.

Machine Gun was standing next to my hiding place. He glanced at me. His face was calm. He nodded his head at me in reassurance. "We are going to be okay. I've done this many times," he seemed to say.

I tried to stay calm.

He gave a hand signal. Some of his men raced up and threw grenades into the cluster of advancing Germans. The Germans answered with machine gun fire.

The explosions and gunfire reverberated in the canyon. I covered my ears.

The gunfire continued, now from both sides. Bullets seared the rocks around me.

Ricochets zinged through the air.

I watched Machine Gun with amazement and admiration. With one arm, he handled his gun with mastery and accuracy. The guerillas tossed more grenades. Rocky earth, stones and dirt flew up, mingled with helmets, clothing and body parts from the German soldiers.

Then there was quiet.

The guerillas cautiously came out of hiding. A few moved up the sides of the canyon, where several of the dead Germans lay, and spat on the ground, murmuring words I did not understand. Machine Gun tapped me on the back, cracked his mouth into what could have been a smile, and shouted an order. Time to move out. None of the guerillas had been hit.

As we marched, I took a good look at the people who had just saved my life.

Their clothes were worn and ragged.

Their faces and eyes were dark and intense.

Most of the men had beards, the rest had several days of unshaven growth.

The women were dressed like the men, with their hair hidden under army style hats.

All could climb like antelopes, as I would find out as our journey together continued.

From time to time, one of them would glance back to make sure we were not followed.

I wondered what cause they were fighting for? All I knew was, at that moment, they were not against me. I was extremely thankful for that.

At this stage of the war, Yugoslavia was divided into several cliques of guerilla warfare.

The main bands were the Partisans of Tito and the Chetniks of Mihailovic.

After April 17, 1941, when Yugoslav's High Command surrendered to the Germans at Sarajevo, Bosnia Herzegovina, Col. Draza Mihailovic and his band of mainly Serbian rebels reached Ravna Gora on the western slopes of the Suvobor Mountains in Serbia, and there he established his headquarters. The Allies supported the resistance movement led by Mihailovic.

The Germans responded by forming the Prinz Eugene SS Division to engage the resistance movements. The SS troops in Prinz Eugene massacred Serbian civilians as collective punishment for supporting resistance movements. Entire Serbian orthodox villages were burned down and the inhabitants – men, women, and children – were shot.

The harsh German occupation left the Serbs in a dilemma. Some wanted a temporary armistice with Germany to end the reprisal massacres of Serbs. From the first days of German occupation, there was spontaneous resistance in Serbia that led to reprisals in which Germans executed many Serbs. Others wanted to keep fighting, the course preferred by the British. Mihailovic decided to keep his forces intact and wait for the Allied landing. However, as it became evident that his guerillas were not pursuing an aggressive campaign, British aid began to shift to the other branch of the Yugoslav resistance: the communist-led Partisans.

Josip Bronz, a Croat-Slovene known first as "Walter" and then as "Tito," was a sergeant in the Austro-Hungarian army and fought against the Serbian army during World War I. Bronz became a POW in Russia, where he adopted the policies of the Bolshevik Regime of Vladimir Stalin, returning to Yugoslavia a staunch communist. He eventually became the Secretary General of the Communist Party in Yugoslavia.

When the country fell apart in 1941, Tito saw an opportunity to seize power. There was little Partisan activity in the fall of Yugoslavia in April 1941, and the surprise German attack on the USSR in June. It was evident that the communists gathered their strength until the USSR was in danger.

Partisan activity began in Northwest Serbia using mines and committing acts of sabotage against bridges and telephone lines. There were additional attacks on convoys and raids on police stations and banks to obtain arms and money.

The Germans treated the Partisans as criminals. They took no prisoners and punished civilian populations suspected of helping Partisans.

The Partisans also discarded the laws of war. They attacked German hospitals and ambulance convoys, and stole medical supplies after killing wounded Germans.

They also adopted the no prisoner policy.

So Yugoslavia was a country divided: Mihailovic made clear his Serbian politics and anti-communist stance. He considered Tito a traitor and a threat to a Serbian-run Yugoslavian kingdom, and felt his immediate duty was to crush him. In his zeal to do so, he made a deal with the Germans, offering a truce in return for arms and the commitment to fight Tito.

As the fight between the two factions escalated, the Partisans moved out of Serbia and made their main base in the high mountains of Bosnia. They remained there during most of the war.

The Chetniks remained in Serbia during the rest of the occupation and maintained truces with the Germans and Italians.

By 1943, the Partisans had 60,000 men in the field. When Italy left the war, Tito's forces seized the weapons of six Italian divisions. Two other Italian divisions joined the Partisan forces. Partisan armed strength rose to 200,000 when Churchill decided to back Tito instead of Mihailovic. By the end of 1944, their numbers were 400,000. A British General was attached to Tito's headquarters as liaison.

I was now traveling with a small band of rebels. They did not speak English, and though I still did not know where they were leading me, I felt relatively safe. I noticed the bite of the freezing air and the weariness of my body. I did not know how much farther they would travel this day, but I hoped it would not be far to food and shelter. I was not sure my strength would hold up much longer.

I felt the last remains of warmth from the now-setting sun on my right shoulder. Its rays created a glowing palette of colors in low-hanging clouds on the horizon: lavender, orange, and brilliant yellow.

The sun set on this day, a day I had been as close to my own death as I had ever been.

I turned my face away from the painful joy of that sunset, a sunset I almost missed, and faced the growing twilight in front of us.

CHAPTER 5

German Fury

The sun sank below the horizon. In the German occupied valley, there was anxiety: one of the patrols had failed to report back to the barracks of the Prinz Eugene SS Division.

Though it was quickly growing dark, a rescue team was dispatched from the base to search for the missing team.

The rescuers covered the few miles to the canyon, arriving just before darkness; there they discovered the lifeless, mutilated bodies of their fallen comrades. Filled with fury, they radioed their base and heard what they wanted to hear: follow the rebels and kill them. And kill any Americans they are harboring.

I looked behind me. Our footsteps in the snow led back down to the distant canyon. They could be clearly seen leading away in the deepening dusk.

On my right, tiny lights blinked in the valley down the slope from the canyon: a camp where Germans were garrisoned. We marched on as night overtook us, and my weariness grew.

After some hours, we came up onto a saddle near

the top of a snow-covered mountain.

There were no clouds in the sky, and the moon had risen, mute and half round, above us.

As we headed down the other side of the mountains, the snow now glistened pale blue in the moonlight, from the glittering crystals at my feet to the shimmering expanse on the plains below.

I wondered about my friends, the crew of Maggie's Drawers. Were they dead or alive? Were they free or captured? Were the Germans even now interrogating them, or were they like me, trudging through the snow somewhere in these mountains? Or were their bodies back at the foot of the mountains?

My feet slipped on the icy snow as I tried to keep up with my protectors.

They were walking fast. They knew what I did not: the Germans were after us.

We walked long into the night trying to put distance between our pursuers and ourselves.

As the hours passed, the only sound was that of our labored breathing and the crunch of our boots in the snow. My legs and body ached. I desperately wanted to sit down and rest. But the rebels were tireless and had no intention of stopping. Once in a while, one of them would glance back to be sure that I was following.

It was near midnight when I saw a scattering of lights ahead and to my left, near the middle slope we were traversing. The rebels headed toward them. Soon we were entering a village etched on the rocky surface of the mountains, hidden among trees.

As we walked down the narrow, snow-covered streets, the rebels were greeted with evident relief.

Women reached out to clasp their hands.

Men called to them from the doorsteps of the humble homes we passed. There were about a hundred people in the village, all dressed in heavy winter coats and hats.

I was led to a large hall in a building in the middle of the village. It was plain inside, with exposed beams and a brushed dirt floor.

There was a wood-burning stove in the center and the entire space was draped in warmth.

There was a desk with a few faded, leather chairs, and a stairway leading to an upstairs floor.

Guns and ammunition rested against one of the walls.

I was offered one of the leather chairs and sank into it gratefully. I closed my eyes and drank in the warmth of the stove.

I would have drifted off to sleep, but the door soon opened again with a blast of cold air, and there was George Morell, escorted by two rebels. As he came in and we exchanged a hearty handshake, the door opened again and in came William Birchfield, John Reilly, Arthur Fleming, O'Connor, Joe Maloney, Clark Fetterman, and Clarence Jensen. They were all exhausted and cold, but alive.

The crew of Maggie's Drawers was reunited, all

except our pilot, Fred Stryker.

Reilly said he saw Fred parachute out of the plane, but lost track of him on the ground. Others confirmed they had seen Fred escape the flaming B-24.

We hoped for the best as we gathered around the stove and exchanged stories.

The rebels had rescued every one of us from German capture and, looking around at each other as we talked, we knew we were lucky to be alive. As time passed, our talk gradually faded and we fell into our own thoughts of the day we had survived and what might lie ahead of us tomorrow.

The rebels had been talking quietly among themselves during our reunion. Once we were settled in, they offered us a bowl of polenta and a cup of water to wash it down. We tore into the meal hungrily; we had gone many hours without eating and so, too, it appeared, had our rescuers. After collecting our bowls and cups, the rebels indicated we should get some rest. We stretched out on the floor around the room, and soon we were all asleep.

Around 3 a.m. our slumber was interrupted by the sound of the door opening and another blast of cold air. Two rebels came in carrying a stretcher. On the stretcher was Fred, our pilot. He was conscious and he gasped and grimaced with pain as the rebels lifted him into a chair. His ankles were swollen like large potatoes.

He exhaled slowly, opened his eyes and looked around, taking in the expressions of worry and concern on our faces. "You look like a bunch of barn owls gaping and stretching your necks," he grimaced. Pain was in his eyes but a smile was on his face, as he said how glad he was to find the whole crew had escaped capture.

We relaxed and patted him on the shoulders, crowding around him. "Watch the feet! Watch the feet!" he asserted.

It turned out Fred had had a rough landing, courtesy of snow-covered rocks that dislocated both his ankles. He could not stand, let alone walk, and had lain helpless, feeling like a prize in an odd game, as he watched the Germans and the rebels scramble toward him. Thankfully, the rebels reached him first.

They had taken turns carrying Fred on their backs as they ran, exchanging gunfire with the Germans. They had succeeded in ridding themselves of their pursuers, and continued on several more miles before they were able to slacken their pace.

Once they felt they were relatively safe, the rebels assembled a stretcher, fashioning it with branches from nearby trees. They placed Fred on the make-shift stretcher and carried him over the mountains and down into the little village.

I glanced over to the rebels as they entered and departed the room.

Their faces were hardened and determined: men and women who had become accustomed to hunger, cold, and life on the run.

Their passionate spirits were rooted in the wild,

rocky earth of their home, and they clung to it and protected it fiercely. Their faces seemed to say, "We will fight, here and now."

One of the rebels, followed by a villager, approached our group, which was huddled around Fred. The man from the village knelt down by Fred's feet and gingerly pressed his fingers into the flesh around his feet and ankles. He seemed to be the village doctor.

He looked up at Fred's face and then reached out to pat his hand in a gesture of reassurance. He uttered a few orders in a low voice to the rebels who looked on. They signaled to us to help them hold Fred down. Five of us held him tightly by the arms, legs and body. Fred took a deep breath and nodded at the doctor.

The doctor grasped the heels and arch of Fred's foot and quickly jerked on it. There was a cracking noise and Fred yelled. The doctor did not waste any time. He immediately moved to the other foot and repeated the procedure; before Fred could even take another breath the other ankle had also been set back into place.

Fred slumped down, sweating and breathing heavily. I said, "It's okay Fred, it's over." He slowly opened his eyes. I saw a wisp of relief as it wafted in his eyes. Then his eyes closed with a heavy sigh.

Suddenly, an explosion ripped through the night. Everyone in the room, except Fred, who was nearly unconscious, jumped at the sound of mortar shells hitting the mountain.

Several rebels rushed into the room from outside; they grabbed their gear and guns and signaled to us that it was time to leave.

We put Fred back on the stretcher and moved out following the rebels.

Outside, mortar shells fell above and below the village. They were coming from the other side of the mountain. Some hit the top of the mountain, sending rocks careening into the houses and buildings. Others passed over the village and onto the slopes of the mountain on the opposite side of the narrow, uninhabited valley below us.

The Germans were trying to shell the village from the valley we had left behind, but the village was protected in the lee of the mountain. We moved out into the dark, hurrying through the village and out onto the mountain side. We hunched down as rocks rained down upon us from the mountain and explosions flashed white light on the faces of the rebels and our crew.

Fred moaned in his dark dreams of semi-consciousness.

A faint gray light was appearing to the east above the rim of dark mountains to our left. I thought I heard the crow of a rooster as we left the village behind us.

There were fifteen of us. Five were rebels, four of whom I had not seen before, and one familiar face, the face of Machine Gun who again led our group. The rest were the crewmen of Maggie's Drawers. We were traveling fast, nearly at a run. A morning frost covered the trees and shrubs and added a glistening layer to the days-old snow.

Once out of the range of artillery, we headed for the upper reaches of the mountain, staying just below the ridge, and fled along the steep slopes. We had been traveling about half an hour when the sounds of the exploding artillery stopped.

We glanced at each other, but kept up our pace.

The soles of my heated boots were beginning to break away; they weren't made for a long trek by foot.

The fiery edge of the sun was now showing over the mountains.

The air temperature began to warm, imperceptibly at first, then more noticeably.

The sound of measured drips came from the trees as the snow began to slowly melt.

Our breath still clouded in the air.

Then we heard the sound of machine gun fire in the distance, in the village we had left behind. The crew of Maggie's Drawers all hesitated a second, looking back. The rebels grabbed our arms, shook their heads and urged us to move on. The next sound we heard was the sound of German aircraft. The Germans were attacking the village by air and land. Now, listening to the sounds of the attack, I thought of the rebels who had saved my life yesterday, the ones who had fed me polenta, and I thought of the men and women who greeted the rebels when we had entered the village earlier.

I prayed that they would be able to escape alive.

It was my turn to help carry Fred; as I took hold of the stretcher I saw that he was awake, and he said, "I am sorry you guys have to carry me."

"Don't worry about it Fred. We're all in this together," I replied. I knew that none of us would be alive if Fred hadn't managed to keep the plane in the air long enough for us to bail out. He was the real hero among us, the last one out of the plane.

As we traveled, we came to understand that the guerillas were holding the mountains of Yugoslavia, while the Germans occupied the valleys.

The Germans could and did enter the mountains, but at high risk of being killed.

They did not have enough troops to secure the mountains and retain control of the valleys.

As we marched on, the sun rose into a bank of clouds that was spread across the sky from horizon to horizon.

Fred dozed, and everyone tramped on silently, each lost in his own thoughts.

The sun was near its zenith, though veiled by a thick layer of clouds, when we heard the sound of a plane, some where far behind us. Machine Gun yelled an order and signaled for us to take cover. I was no longer carrying Fred, and ran into the shadow of a large boulder and froze there like a frightened rabbit.

Everyone disappeared into the bushes, behind rocks and under trees.

I held my breath as the German plane flew over us, low and slow.

I did not move a muscle as it went past and seemed to be heading off to continue its search of the mountains.

Then the plane turned, circled and headed toward us again.

They must have spotted us!

The plane approached and time seemed too slow.

I heard the rumble of its engines growing louder.

Sweat ran over my tightly closed eyes and seeped into the corners, stinging. I was frozen in place, braced for bombs and machine gun fire from the air, as I heard it pass right over our heads.

Only when I realized that the sound of the engines had dwindled into the distance did I dare open my eyes. I took a deep breath and sagged against the rock in relief. At a command from Machine Gun, we all staggered out of our hiding places, faces showing strain and relief. Many continued to look apprehensively into the sky as we once again took up our march.

We still did not know where the rebels were taking us, but we had no choice but to follow them and trust their combat skills and their knowledge of the enemy. We were entirely at their mercy, our lives in their hands, and I wondered how many more times they would save our lives or if we were fated to die with them in some remote village in Yugoslavia.

We marched until the sunset. It was our second day behind enemy lines.

CHAPTER 6

Lost, Then and Now

I felt helpless as I followed the strangers on the mountaintops. I was being taken away, and did not know where I was going.

It was like my childhood, when I was lost in the mysterious and strange world of grown up people.

Bill. Bill Kollar is my name.

William M. is how it is stated on my birth certificate and my Army and Air Force records. The rebels ahead of me did not know my name; they did not ask. They just kept on walking, taking me wherever they wished.

I was born in Middleville, Michigan, on March 4, 1920.

Who would have thought that twenty-four years later, I would have feelings of helplessness similar to those of my childhood? That once again my fate would be in the hands of people dragging me along? I was born the youngest child of Harvey and Pearl Kollar. My brother, Harold, was two years older than I, taller and thinner, with lighter hair.

Unlike most people, I cannot recollect my very early years. I don't remember being held, happy, hungry or crying. My memories seem to begin at five when I started first grade. Especially the day that Mother told me I did not have to go to school. My little heart raced with the idea of spending the day outside in the yard rolling my beat-up train through the sand. The neighbors' mutt wandered over for a game of stick toss.

My mother was hanging laundry.

My brother was on his way to school.

Dad had gone to work at the Middleville Cotton Mill. Yes, this was going to be a great day.

Our neighbor, Frank Barnes, came to visit, driving his shiny black open touring car with side curtains. That was nothing unusual. Mr. Barnes often came to visit. He drove past me with a wave and pulled all the way into our garage. Our house, that used to belong to my mom's moth er until her death, was one of the very few houses in town that had an attached garage; most were set a little ways from the house. Mr. Barnes, his wife, and daughter, Elizabeth, had been close friends to our family for some time. Harold, Elizabeth, and I had played hide and seek for end less hours, and many times we spent the night at their home.

I did not think anything out of the ordinary was happening when he and my mother began to pack some of our belongings and put them in the backseat of his car. "Are we going for a ride, Mother?" I asked.

"Yes, Billy," she replied. "We are going for a short trip."

Mother seemed tense as she forced a cheerful expression to keep me from asking too many questions.

"But I want to stay home and play," I begged.

She did not answer me. She was busy throwing clothes and belongings into the backseat of Mr. Barnes' car. Then she tossed me on top of all the clothes in the backseat, and we sped west, leaving behind a cloud of dust.

I looked out the back window of the car. My train lay motionless on the sand.

Jake the mutt also lay in our yard, his head resting on his paws. His sad brown eyes watched the car until we were out of sight.

I turned from the back window and snuggled down into the clothes piled high in the backseat of the car. Rain had begun to fall and as we drove the storm intensified. I closed my eyes against the lightning and thunder and the powerful rain that was now beating against the car.

"Mom, please, let's go home," I pleaded once more. "Our home is ahead of us son," she replied.

Finally, the car stopped at a roadside park by the muddy banks of the Grand River.

Mr. Barnes pitched a tent, but the feeling was not that of a fun camping adventure. My mood was as small, damp and uncomfortable as Mr. Barnes' tent. Night fell and we spent the night crowded together in the tent. I missed my bed, my warm room. I missed Harold and I wondered what Dad was thinking about now.

Frank Barnes left in the morning to go to work in the

Lost, Then and Now

city as a motorcycle policeman. When he returned in the late afternoon, he and Mother spent a lot of time together, walking, laughing and holding each other.

They had little time for me. Frank seldom looked at me, let alone spoke to me. For several weeks, I did not go to school, and I spent my time playing by the river. Eventually, Mom entered me into a school about a half mile away. When I asked her when we would be seeing Dad and Harold again, she would answer, "We will see them sometime."

One day when I got home Mom wasn't there. Mr. Barnes did not usually get back to the tent until almost dinnertime. It was still hours before nightfall, yet the day had gone dark. Thick, threatening clouds covered the sky. The wind was blowing, lifting leaves from the ground and twisting them in the air. I sat in the tent door, my arms wrapped around my legs, and my head rested on my knees. I watched the storm approach. The wind gathered force and began to bend the branches of trees.

Rain began to fall. Thunder boomed and lightning splintered the air. I fled inside the tent, button it up and crawled into my blanket.

I lay there for some time as the wind whistled and howled, shaking the tent like a rag.

The storm broke loose and driving rain slashed down on the tent. I heard nearby trees falling. I curled up and closed my eyes and waited to be carried off in the gale. I finally fell into a fitful sleep and dreamed of roaring trains and flashing lights and wailing mothers.

I awoke with a start and looked wildly around. I was relieved to see the tent was still standing and I was still safely in it. I cautiously crawled out of my blanket, unbutton the front door and peered out.

The river was swollen, transformed from a sleepy, green flow to a loud, brown torrent. Fallen trees and debris littered the riverbank.

When Mother and Mr. Barnes came home, I hardly noticed.

The next day, I found a fishing line in the old tool box. Searching the tent, I found a safety pin behind a pile of papers and I twisted it into a hook. I dug some worms from the muddy banks of the river, placed them in an old milk can, and began my favorite pastime.

Sitting on top of a fallen tree, I spent hours fishing. I missed my brother and my dad.

I could not understand why we couldn't drive back to see them.

Little did I know that my mother was hiding from my father.

Frank Barnes bought a bigger tent. Now it was a bit more comfortable, but still muddy and damp.

A couple of months later, when it was sunny and dry, my mother took me to Hastings, Michigan. We walked into a big white building. Mother talked to a few people, picked up some papers and wrote a few things on them. On the way out, I asked my mother "What are we doing here, Mom?"

"I just filed for divorce from your father," she said.

Her divorce was granted.

Mother got custody of me. Father got custody of Harold.

These were traumatic years for me.

I missed my older brother terribly.

I never got used to living in a tent.

I wanted my home, my friends to play with.

These were the things I thought about as I followed the rebels through the Yugoslavian mountains. My youth hardened me to believe only in what you could see for yourself. I got used to hard knocks early in life. Not knowing where I was going did not really scare me, although I did have concerns.

I had the childhood of a transient. I went to five schools in the first grade alone.

I failed and had to be held back and repeat the first grade. I really missed Miss Ellwood, my first grade teacher back in Middleville. I longed for just one teacher who could get to know me, without giving up on me and sitting me in the back of the room because I couldn't keep up with the rest of the students.

While other kids fell asleep at night in their warm beds, with full stomachs, dreaming of fun games and toys, I dreamed of a home, my dad, and Harold.

Now as I was led through strange lands I once again yearned for the warmth of home, bed, family and food, any food in any amount.

The Last Mission

Billy Kollar, age five
Middleville, Mich. in front yard

Lost, Then and Now

Billy, with brother Harold and Mother

CHAPTER 7

On The Run

The trails leading up and down the mountains were seldom marked, as far as I could tell, but the rebels seemed to know the terrain well and seldom faltered in their march.

It was early spring.

At lower altitudes, green blades of grass were pushing up and the wildflowers peeped from beneath the stones. Trees were blossoming. Birds were coming back on the heels of winter. Up in the high passes, the snow was beginning to melt.

The smells of spring were carried on the strong breeze even up to the high trails we climbed.

Two days had passed, two days of climbing mountains and trekking through the woods with no food and very little water. We often dug in a snow bank to get some clean snow to eat to quench our thirst.

The rebels had small teams stationed at strategic lookout posts throughout the mountains.

When we'd reached one of these posts, our team of escorts would change – fresh legs for tired ones.

We said good-bye to Machine Gun at one of these outposts.

We had rested a few minutes, and when the rebels motioned to us that it was time to depart, Machine Gun did not don his gear. It took me a moment to realize that he was staying behind. He looked at me gravely, and I gazed back, not knowing how to thank this man.

Finally, I rose to my feet and saluted the man who helped save me and had traveled so far with my crew. His eyes shone as he returned the gesture in rebel fashion: his fist tapped on his chest above his heart. We turned and headed off once again into the mountains.

Our destination still remained unrevealed by our guides. As far as we knew, none of them spoke English and we did not see them take out any maps where we might have been able to get a glimpse of our location. For purposes of necessity and survival we placed a blind trust in these people and trudged on.

The weather had warmed enough to make our flight suits uncomfortably warm during the day. My feet began to sweat as my boots heated up. The soles were now flapping freely and when they stuck to my sweaty feet they caused me to trip. However, after the sun went down the temperature dropped dramatically, and the nights were freezing. I would lie on the ground and shiver in my suit, pulling the collar up around my chin.

We Americans talked little among ourselves; it was necessary to save most of our strength for the march. The silence was occasionally broken by Fred who would say,

"Let me walk, please, I can walk." When we would

stop, he would try to place his feet on the ground to stand, but then he would collapse in pain and frustration.

We walked on.

The third day I was carrying the back of Fred's stretcher. Every step I took was an effort. I could hardly keep my balance because of the tripping, flapping, soles of my boots. George was carrying the front of the stretcher. "George, hold up."

We stopped and placed the stretcher on the ground. I unfastened my boots, took them off and held them up. The sun glinted through the gaping holes between the soles and uppers. I threw the boots off into the rocks and brush at the side of the trail.

"You can't walk barefoot," Fred declared.

"I can't walk with those boots," I replied.

I was inspecting what was left of my socks when I heard a grunt and George called out, "Fred!" I looked over and Fred had rolled off the stretcher onto the wet ground. As I watched, he slowly lifted himself up, holding onto the trunk of a tree. His face was set in determination. When he was standing he managed a grim smile.

"I am going to walk," he stated.

Fred was of German descent and he delighted in telling us he was "going to dump us into the 'fatherland'" when our mission took us over Germany. The crew just laughed, knowing that Fred was from Pennsylvania.

Now, we walked side by side, me in my socks, Fred with his cane.

It was not long before sharp rocks and thorns had cut my feet and torn more holes in my socks and I wondered if I had been rash in throwing away my boots. Fred's ankles began to swell again, and within a few hours they ballooned to twice their normal size.

I looked around me. Everyone on our team was tired, thirsty and hungry. The rebels never seemed to have food – even at their outposts. Our faces were red with exertion. I finally borrowed a knife and cut the legs off of my flight suit. I couldn't stand the heat anymore. I was rewarded with a mild breeze against my bare flesh.

The sun began to sink behind the peaks of the mountains. We turned a corner of the trail and I saw ahead a tiny village on the slope below us.

There were only a few homes, and they were all dark.

We were guided through the narrow, deserted streets and taken into a room of one of the houses.

Someone brought us polenta and water.

A woman came in, and, bathing a cloth in a basin, washed the blood from my feet. Suddenly the door flew open and a man entered.

"Hey boys! How are you?"

At first I could not believe what I was hearing. English! One of the rebels in the tiny village spoke English.

We all began firing questions at him, which he attempted to answer in his thick accent.

He was a man of medium height, about 50 years old, dressed in the familiar dark, heavy clothes. He had a black beard, a black cap, and bright, black eyes. He tended to smile as he answered our questions.

"Ya. Ya. Tito's," he said pointing to himself and the other rebels. This confirmed what we had thought: these were the Partisans of Tito. He told us they were trying to take us to a place where we could be airlifted back to our base. He said we had a long way to go before reaching what he called the "Valley of Freedom."

"I lived in America," he proclaimed proudly. "In Michigan."

"Michigan?" I answered, "I'm from Michigan." "What your name?" he asked. He was the first rebel to ask any of us our names.

"William, William Kollar, what is yours?" "I name Goran."

Goran had lived in Michigan in the early twenties. He worked in the steel mills, and while he was there he got into a barroom brawl and killed a man. He ran away from the law and did not stop running until he reached the mountains of Yugoslavia.

He looked at my feet and said, "I find boots for you." A while later he came back holding a pair of military, nail-studded mountain climbing boots and a pair of thick khaki socks. I felt as though it was Christmas and I had gotten the gift I had always wanted.

Smiling, I slipped the socks and boots on my feet.

They were a bit tight, but far better than walking barefoot. "Thank you!" I exclaimed, pumping his hand in gratitude.

"Okay friend, good, good," he assured me while tapping me on the shoulder.

"You leave soon," he said, and explained that we had to cross the next valley that night. He told us that in the valley was a German-held town that we would have to pass undetected.

"Will be dark, Germans not see you," Goran said. "Must be very quiet, like mice," he smiled as he walked his fingers through the air between us.

Not long after that, we were ordered to move out. Goran waved to us as we left, and I wished he were going with us.

But soon, the village was far behind as we worked our way down to the valley. Apparently, we had to cross this valley to get to the next relatively safe mountain range. We moved along quietly. One of the Partisans walked some distance ahead of us, scouting the territory.

We were almost to the foot of the mountain when the scout came back carrying a flashlight wrapped in a cloth to dim its light.

The rebels gathered around him and began to talk, several of them making hand gestures in different directions.

This was bad news. The Partisans didn't talk much unless there was a problem to solve.

They signaled for us to move on, parallel to the mountains, toward the town. We forged forward along the trail. Then, in the dim light of a quarter moon, we could see the road, a road that we had to cross, and now we could see the problem. A large convoy of German trucks was growling along the road using only blackout lights. The trucks were probably carrying ammunition, food and medical supplies, and possibly, army troops.

They were running in blackout for their own protection.

We made our way down to within a few yards of the road. There, we were motioned to sit down and wait. The convoy was moving very slowly and finally came to a halt. I could see faint images of the trucks, illuminated by their slight blackout lights, and soon men jumped out of the cabs. Most headed off toward the rear of the convoy where the ration truck was, but about a half dozen stayed behind and spread out to guard the convoy.

With hand gestures, the rebels made us understand we were to run between the trucks, one man at a time, and reunite on the other side several yards from the road. It was about 25 yards from where we sat to the other side of the road.

I watched as two of the rebels, and then three of our crewmen, ran across the road, one by one. Then another rebel rose with his arm around Fred's waist to help support him.

Fred half-ran and was half-pulled to the other side. When I saw their shadows disappear into the darkness on the other side of the road, I sighed in relief. Then one of the remaining rebels tapped me on the shoulder signifying that it was my turn. I ran.

I ran downward a few feet from the trucks. The shoulder of the road fell away sharply under my feet, and my right foot caught in an ironwood bush. I jerked my leg while still running. A ripping sensation and a searing pain tore through the right side of my groin. My foot came free, but when I tried to put weight on it, I felt an excruciating pain. My right leg crumpled under me and I fell on my back hard. I saw stars in the now overcast sky.

I rolled over onto my stomach and looked around anxiously to see if I had attracted any attention.

The Germans still had their guns slung casually on their shoulders.

With a stifled groan, I rose to my feet and stumbled toward the road, half-dragging my right leg. Finally, I reached the other side and stumbled down a shallow embankment into the arms of Clark. I collapsed in agony as we waited in tense silence for the rest of the crew and guerillas to make it across the road.

When we were all gathered again, the silent command was made to move out. I clenched my teeth against the extreme pain, and limped forward.

The town was dark and wrapped in silence: a black out to prevent Allied bombers from seeing it.

The moon was now hiding behind the clouds. We formed a single file line, holding onto the shirt of the person ahead of us to avoid getting lost in the pitch-black night.

My head and groin ached. It was extremely difficult to walk.

The Partisan with the muffled flashlight led the way, and the rest of us followed, shuffling along like a giant caterpillar, crawling in and out between buildings, freezing when dogs barked. The flashlight appeared and disappeared as the leader turned corners and skirted backyards. We were nearly out of town when a door opened, casting a dim beam of light into the night. A German officer swaggered out of the door, clutching the hand of a woman. Both were laughing, perhaps drunk.

We were just across the street, and the dim light seemed as bright as a searchlight.

We froze and dared not breathe.

The door slammed shut and the man and woman walked unsteadily down the road, not 25 feet from us.

We were pressed against the side of a building, and for one moment, whether due to intuition or some slight noise, the officer seemed to look intently in our direction, but was soon distracted by the woman pulling on his hand. She led him away, and we stole off into the night and out of town.

Once free from the town, someone cut me a cane from an ironwood bush.

We came to a railroad track and followed it for a mile to a bridge that crossed a river.

On the other side of the river, we sat and rested.

Two of the guerillas headed back down the railroad track.

We were still catching our breath and sipping our rationed water when several explosions rocked the night air.

My companions jumped to their feet. The two guerillas were running back and we all rushed up the mountainside as sirens howled behind us.

The guerillas had blown up the railroad bridge; it was still ablaze with their handiwork.

The sky was flooded with light as the Germans searched the skies for aircraft. When none were found, the anti-aircraft floodlights turned to the hillside where we were making our way upward.

The guerillas were lightfooted and sure as they climbed the mountain face; we followed the best we could as the searchlights closed in on us.

I closed my eyes against the sharp pain in my thigh and groin. The sounds of men breathing hard while climbing surrounded me. The searchlights were bearing down on us.

"Sakrij se!" ("Hide!") yelled our leader.

Even those who didn't speak the language knew he was telling us to hide. We jumped behind boulders and trees and froze, just as the giant swath of light washed over us. As soon as it passed by, we ran again, just behind the path of light flying along the hillside, but we angled our course upward. The light had blinded us and we stumbled, catching ourselves with our hands against the ground. We had run several hundred yards when we saw the lights coming back toward us. We ran until almost the last moment.

"Sakrij se!"

Once again, we all ducked down and held still. The light briefly illuminated the hillside; its bright white light in stark contrast to the night. We felt naked and exposed to the hunters in the valley.

The lights passed on; they were searching behind us again. We ran, frequently looking back over our shoulders.

In this manner, fleeing in the dark and hiding from the light, we made our way up the mountainside into the thick forest and away from the valley. We dodged the ever sweeping beams until the searchlights could no longer reach us. Then, we ran another half mile just to be safe.

We went over a low ridge, and on the far side of the ridge, high up on the mountain, our group collapsed on the ground. The guerillas were not particularly out of breath, but they seemed relieved and I hoped that this meant we were out of danger for the moment.

"I can't believe they blew that bridge with us sitting right there!" Fred gasped in astonishment.

"Man, I wish I could run faster if they're going to pull stunts like that," I said. I was lying on the ground, breathing hard, eyes closed, talking up to the sky.

The rebels took a small drink of water and signaled for us to do the same. We rested a few minutes more and then began walking, still headed up the side of the mountain.

On The Run

Bill, at the air depot of Albuquerque, New Mexico 1942

"Pee-Wee" Fleming standing by the plane that crashed in the airfield of Lecce, just missing our tent

William Birchfield and an Italian houseboy taking away an army cot from the British. Army cots were a hot commodity in Lecce.

Living quarters in Lecce, Italy. Bill's tent is the white one in the foreground. Since there was a shortage of American tents, he had to take one away from the British.

CHAPTER 8

Pain, a Constant Companion

After about two hours, we stopped in a roughly circular clearing between thick trunks of trees. The night was cloudy and cold, and the group was so weary with physical exertion and mental strain that sleep came quickly to everyone.

For me, the climb had been excruciating.

Spasms of pain racked my body radiating from my groin, where the pain was concentrated, to my limbs and my guts. The ache made its way to my eyes, and my head.

Every time I stepped on the uneven surface, a charge orbited through my body.

Behind me, sounds of alarms, searchlights waving in the darkness, voices yelling in the distance.

Ahead of me, ground ascending to the darkness, to the unknown. Light-footed rebels running away from danger. Behind me was the havoc that had followed the explosions. We could hear the excited barking of the German tracking dogs looking for our scent.

Ahead of me was darkness, and safety.

I had no choice but to move ahead and live with the pain.

Pain, a Constant Companion

I had gritted my teeth, planted my cane on the ground, and lifted myself up, toward the rebels who were looking back to make sure I was following.

Now as night had fallen and I lay on the cold, hard ground, I thought back to my childhood. Then, it had been Mother and Frank who occasionally glanced back to see if I was following, not seeing the mental pain coursing through my small body. I knew pain then, too. Mental torment, was a constant companion.

A child living in confusion, always on the move, running from the past and moving on to a dark and uncertain future.

After the divorce, Mother and Frank moved into an awful cement blockhouse in Ada, Michigan. My father was now allowed to come and see me and take me away some weekends. Those weekends were the happiest moments of my young life.

For a few days, my heart would replenish with the joy and security that my father's presence afforded.

One weekend when Father came to pick me up, I was wearing a new overcoat, one that Mother had made for me. I was proud of the new overcoat; it made me feel special. I did not often get new clothes.

My father drove up in his new 1926 Model T Ford Coupe. As I saw it approaching along the dirt road, I jumped for joy, anticipating the ride and the time I would spend with my father.

My joy wore out a bit when I saw that Grandma Lou

Lanting was riding in the passenger seat. It was not that I disliked my stepgrandma, but that I would have to share the seat with her – all 300 pounds of her. Grandma's lap became my seat. Her large body left little room for me. My head was pressed almost against the ceiling.

Shortly after we left my mother's cement block house, sprinkles began to fall from the sky. Despite the discomfort of sharing a seat with Grandma, I was very happy.

I watched my dad with pride and admiration, as he drove his new car. He told me stories, and spoke of my brother. Father turned to look at me and smiled once in a while.

"Watch the road, Harvey," Grandma ordered with her authoritative voice. Father minded her until he knew she was not watching, then he turned and winked at me, and we both smiled.

By the time we got to Grand Rapids, the rain was coming down hard and it was difficult to see the road ahead. Father was driving with one hand because he was using the other hand to operate the manual windshield wiper.

The downpour continued and they tried in vain to read the cross-street signs obscured by the rain. They were looking for a street named Pearl.

The search in the downpour continued.

I was tired and cold. Squeezed between my grandmother and the hard car top, I was increasingly uncomfortable. Grandma's labored breath blew across my face with a smell of stale beer, which nauseated me.

Please, please, I begged, let them find Pearl Street. I wanted this ride to come to an end. "There," yelled Grandma. "There is Pearl." She pointed to the right.

Father was looking to the left. He reacted quickly, instinctively turning the car to the right. Suddenly, the car broke over a little knoll, swung to the left, to the right, and to the left again. Then it began to skid on the wet street.

"Watch out! Watch out!" I heard terror in Grandma's voice.

Directly in front of us was a high concrete abutment where the road dead ended. We were probably going about thirty miles per hour when we hit the abutment straight on. The car came to an abrupt halt. Sounds of shattering glass and crushing metal disturbed the quiet neighborhood. Waves of flesh and fat from Grandma's body propelled me through the windshield. I rolled over the hood and fender and onto the muddy street.

Rain poured onto my body and my face.

Then darkness. I knew I was not dead. I was just blinded by the blood flowing into my eyes from the deep cuts above each of my eyebrows.

Father rushed to pick me up. "Are you okay, son?"

I heard cars stopping. Someone picked me up and put me into the backseat of a brand new Buick that rushed me to the hospital. Blood spattered onto the clean seat of the car. My father was trying to stop the bleeding with his handkerchief. The blood was cleared from my eyes. Between my eyelids, I observed my dad's face worrying about me.

"I am okay, Dad," I said reassuringly.

Through his ripped shirt, I saw on his chest the black and blue imprint of the steering wheel.

"We are almost to the hospital," said the kind voice of the man driving the car.

Grandma was not with us.

Thank God I had room to breathe.

She was spared without a scratch. Apparently, her body had enough natural padding to protect her.

Later in life, I always associated Grandma with the invention of air bags.

"You are fortunate to have hit that abutment. That prevented you from dropping six hundred feet over the hill," the driver told us.

Dad was not able to fix his car and we took a taxi to Uncle Clyde's house.

I was heartbroken because my new, beautiful over coat was torn and bloodstained beyond repair.

Dad waited until after my stitches were removed to take me back to my mother. My mother was unhappy to say the least. She gave Father an earful. My dad listened without saying anything. At the end he apologized. But Mother said that he would never take me again. I was terrified at that thought.

"No Mom, I am okay. It wasn't Dad's fault."

"We'll see," she said and turned around, pulling my hand, and dragging me into the cement blockhouse.

I looked back over my shoulder and winked at my

dad. He winked back. We both smiled, knowing that Mother would eventually soften up.

An eerie feeling overcame me as I lay atop the mountain, resting before another day's walk.

The voices of the Germans remained as faded echoes.

The searchlights had been erased in the darkness.

The moon bashfully pulled over the clouds, enough to see the outline of the man I was sleeping beside.

I felt the chill of the night in my legs. This was going to be another cold night, one among the ghosts of the past, one among the images of the future.

It was hours past midnight. Melancholy overcame my heart.

"What is this all about?" I wondered.

Humans were running like hunted animals, killing one another, and for what? In the name of peace? In the name of democracy? In the name of communism?

For freedom, of course!

The howl of a wolf sounded off over the horizon.

I had to block out the pain and the cold to get some badly needed sleep.

The morning would be here shortly and the marathon walk would continue once again.

I closed my eyes, dreaming of my warm, brand new overcoat that Mother once made for me.

The Last Mission

Billy playing with the puppy, after his Mother gave him a haircut.

Pain, a Constant Companion

CHAPTER 9

Lost in the Mountains

I was exhausted, but each time I drifted off, a sharp pain in my groin and leg wakened me. My body felt as though it was riddled with needles, and though I couldn't keep my eyes open – the lids felt thick and weighted with fatigue deep sleep continued to elude me.

"Please, God, let me rest for just a moment or two."

The sky was profoundly dark, and the night air was bitter cold and very still – not a breath of air was moving.

I could hear men snoring. All around the clearing they were curled into tight balls against the cold.

The man next to me was mumbling in his sleep: he spoke of food, fishing and telephones, only God knows what he was dreaming about.

I drifted between pain and twilight sleep: through visions of warm sun; along beaches crowded with vacationing families; into restaurants where I sat with a beautiful woman at a linen-covered table and was served luxurious, rich foods; in clean, tiled showers with fresh-smelling soap and dry, fluffy towels; in soft feather beds with crisp, cool sheets and slippers nearby.

All this I saw, and all this was shattered each time I

moved, even slightly, and searing pain blazed across my nerves.

Groans did not escape me, but only because I bit my lip bloody.

The sky to the east turned ash gray. Soon, rays of sunlight would fan up into the sky from the mountaintop. The man next to me moved. A slight, unconscious grunt came from his throat. He stretched out his legs, throwing an arm over his face. It was Fred. He blinked his eyes, stared up into the sky for a moment, and then turned to look at me. His face registered concern.

"Bill, are you okay?"

"Sure. I just want to get moving." "Me, too. Did you get any sleep?"

I smiled and grimaced as the pain shot through me once more. Even though he outranked me, Fred and I had spent some off-duty time together drinking and dreaming in the town near the base at Lecce.

The sky was now blazing red, and the fiery edge of the sun was burning over the line of peaks to our left. As beams of light punctured the shadow of our protected hollow, the group began to stir: drowsy voices, irritable exclamations, and yawns. Fred and I struggled to get up. I pulled myself up by grasping a tree trunk, and then leaned against the tree for support; Fred leaned heavily on his cane. We looked at each other, shook our heads and smiled grimly.

"Well, we're quite a mess aren't we?" he said.

I borrowed a knife from one of the rebels and cut a ring around the top of my cane.

I was gingerly trying to put my weight on my right leg when William came over to me.

"Come on, Bill, I'll help you walk."

William Birchfield, our navigator, was about 5 feet 5 inches tall. He was lean and strong. He, too, treated all enlisted men as equals; he was well liked and respected.

"Thanks, William, but I think I can make it." I used my hand to move my right leg forward, then hopped on my left leg.

Push, hop, push, hop, I made my way after the crew. William looked after me doubtfully but did not insist. I did not want to slow anyone down and declined help from Clark Fetterman a little while later.

As the day wore on, I was able to put a little more weight on my right leg and could take a step without using my hand to help move my leg forward.

I was flushed and sweating profusely despite the cool temperature of the day.

Every little rock or pebble in my path caused nearly unbearable pain if my foot hit it, but somehow I kept pace with the rest of the team. We stopped to rest every few hours, and I welcomed the chance to catch my breath.

We worked our way down the backside of the mountain, still heading south, and then traversed a small valley.

In the valley, greenery had pierced the earth, newly warm with thin spring sunshine. There were tender grass shoots, poppies and wild daisies.

By the time we were halfway up the next mountain,

the sun was setting.

I fallowed the team with dogged determination, hardly aware of moving, hardly aware of their occasional questions. I kept putting one foot in front of the other, my mind blank, my body on automatic pilot.

The miles slipped by; every step took me a bit closer to freedom, a bit closer to home. I was weak and dizzy from hunger, and my clothes fit more loosely than they had just four days ago, but my feet kept moving. I was grateful for the simple act of hopping on my left foot. I pushed my other leg forward with my right hand. Slowly I made my way. Slowly home drew nearer: inches at a time. I could not give up.

I was hardly aware when our guides called for a halt. It was dark. My body buckled under the weight of weariness; I fell to my hands and knees, head hanging between my arms, then I rolled slowly over on my back.

I closed my eyes and knew no more.

Water splashed on my face and I opened my eyes, startled.

Surely I was dreaming.

But there it was again – splat, splat, splat – coming a little faster now.

Fuzzy thoughts, but I finally realized that a light rain was falling. I sat up. The rest of the group was also rising.

The rain soon became a downpour. We moved toward a rock outcropping with the rebels urging us on. In the night rain, I could see very little: vague shapes and occasional voices surrounded me.

"Stay close! Don't get lost," someone nearby said. I moved toward the voice. It was Fred. He was close behind the guerilla leader.

"Move toward the rocks," he called through the falling rain.

The earth was muddy and I could hear the boots slapping and squishing up the hill.

"Over here! Over here!"

We moved toward the voices and found the rest of the crew of Maggie's Drawers huddled against the slightly overhung boulder.

"Dodi ovamo!" ("Come here!") voices called from a little farther up the hill.

We went toward them and found the rebels in a large hollowed out area making a small cave-like space. We squeezed under it and had a head count. No one was missing. Outside our shelter, the rain was falling hard in the darkness. A melancholy feeling soaked through us as we stood dripping in the black hollow of the cave.

There was no lightning, no thunder, no drama to relieve the pressing force of the powerful downpour. When we turned away from the mouth of the cave, I realized my teeth were chattering.

The rebels had congregated in a corner to share and preserve what warmth they could. We did the same.

I slumped against the rock, men on either side of me, and listened to the rain hitting the ground. Perhaps it was my imagination, but it did not seem to be pounding the earth with as much force as it had been just a few moments earlier.

I closed my eyes, listening intently for any slight sign of the storm slackening, and then I fell asleep.

When I woke, the world was silent. The rain had stopped, and we moved out again, up steep slopes now slippery with mud.

We reached the mountaintop in the wee hours of the morning, started down, and came upon a small village on the other side.

It was a tiny gathering of perhaps a dozen small homes clinging to the side of the mountain. There were a few horses; I wondered how they had managed to keep them from the Germans.

The Germans were ruthless and thorough in their looting, making sure there was nothing left in the villages besides empty houses and hungry people. But the villagers were unconquerable. They could not be cowed and continued to support the rebels with what little they had.

I was led a little way up the hill to one of the homes and directed inside; my companions were taken on to other homes in the village.

The room I entered was bare of furniture. In the center of the space was a large, flat stove, with wood burning on its top. The open fire made the room feel warm and welcoming. I sat on the dirt floor, my feet toward the stove, and fell asleep.

The sounds of footsteps awoke me. An elderly woman dressed in a black dress with a black kerchief covering her head came into the room from outside. She walked toward the fire as I watched through half-opened eyelids.

The room was dark, the only source of light was the slow-burning fire. The woman pushed at the fire with a pair of tongs, moving it toward the center of the stove block. She then wiped the surface of the block with a cloth. She reached into the pocket of her waist apron and pulled something out. I glimpsed a white oval object. She held it between her fingers and with a quick move smacked it against the side of the stove and lifted her hand above the hot stone top.

A stream of clear and yellow liquid fell to the stove top. I heard sizzling.

My eyes were wide open now. My stomach rumbled and my mouth watered. The elderly woman scooped up the egg with a spatula and slid it onto a plate. She turned and walked toward me, her arm extended, offering me the plate: on it was the most beautiful fried egg I had ever seen, and a healthy portion of polenta.

My eyes must have glowed with delight because she chuckled and said "Jedi." ("Eat.") Her eyes were deep, dark and kind.

"Jedi." she repeated, handing me a spoon.

I took the plate. She smiled, toothless and encouraging.

She walked to the door and I was overcome with

Lost in the Mountains

guilt as I looked at the lovely egg and polenta on the beat up tin plate.

It was very likely that this woman was going without food herself in order to feed me.

The door closed behind her and my hunger overcame my guilt. I cut into the egg with the spoon and closed my eyes as the first bite of egg hit my tongue. I chewed slowly, relishing the flavor and texture. I took a bite of polenta and another of egg. As I ate, a warm sensation grew in my body; my eyes closed again and I saw myself in a room full of tables laden with salads, fresh cheeses, and hot bread.

A hand held a silver platter in front of my face, and on it was a giant, perfect egg. "Jedi, jedi," a voice said to me.

"Moramo ici!" ("We must go!") A rebel was standing in the doorway.

I opened my eyes, took my last bite and stood up. I followed the rebel out the door. We went to the center of the village where there was a small square and a hand-operated water pump. The rest of the rebels and the crew of Maggie's Drawers were there.

We all washed our faces and shaved with razors provided by the villagers.

With a content stomach and a fresh shave, I followed the group down the mountain trail with a feeling of renewed vigor.

Billy with Mother

Lost in the Mountains

CHAPTER 10

Rings On My Cane

Rays of the sun shone through the cracks of the old barn, highlighting bits of hay and dust floating there.

My sleep had been restless that morning, even though I was exhausted from walking most of the previous day. We had found this small barn at the far end of the valley and we made it our home for a few hours. Around me the rest of the group still slept, lying on the thin layers of hay. Cautiously, I sat up and tested each of my stiff, sore muscles. I picked up my cane and carved another ring on its tip, keeping track of our days on the run.

I thought back and tried to remember how many days had passed before I began to carve the rings on my cane. My life had become a waking dream of disjointed events: my feet plodding up a mountain; my hands reaching for a taste of polenta; my eyes scanning the horizon for enemies. I had not known I could survive in such circumstances.

I was isolated from the world, not knowing the latest news or how the war was progressing. Each day was an unknown. Where would the end of the day find me? Where would I find myself lying to rest?

I watched as the figures in the dim barn began to stir.

We spent every minute of the day and night together, but there was a minimal exchange of words between us. Everyone was preoccupied with the uncertainty of the future. Yet, we all believed that we would come out of this adventure alive.

George Morell was the first one to get up. I did not know him very well; he was new to our crew. George was our co-pilot and he seemed very cordial, polite, and businesslike. He wore his flight suit and sheep-lined boots the entire time. He came and sat beside me.

"How are you feeling, Bill?" "My leg's a little better."

George pulled a photograph from his left breast pocket. It was a photograph of a woman and a boy. The woman was standing slightly behind the boy, who looked about two years old. She had a bright smile and her eyes looked happy. The boy wore a smiling face.

"My wife and son," he said, "They're back in New Jersey."

"I would like to play one-on-one with him some day." George continued.

"You will, George," I assured him.

"I hope so," he replied as he placed the picture back in his pocket. A tear rolled down his cheek. This was the first emotion I had witnessed from any of the crew. A little humanity entered my heart; tenderness that was forgotten in this inhumane race for survival.

As the rest of the group rose and prepared for another marathon walk, I wondered if everyone was as hungry as I was. We had not eaten since the previous morning, when

I had my egg and polenta.

I stood up. The boots I had been given were holding up well. They had become more pliable and felt comfortable on my feet. We seldom took our boots off; we had to be ready to run at any moment.

I was testing my leg when I realized that my flight suit felt particularly itchy. I had the sensation of small pieces of straw falling down on my chest. I took off the top piece and shook it out. No straw. Then I saw little red bumps on my skin. Bites. Quickly, I searched my jacket and found the culprits, lice. I stripped off my cut-off pants and socks in haste, and noticed other men in the barn were doing the same. All over the room men were jumping up, flinging off clothes, and examining their itchy hides.

"Just what we need, lice!" someone exclaimed.

There was a general chorus of grunts in agreement as we tried to pick our clothes clean of the little infesters. Fred, who was nearby, looked over at John Reilly, and said "The lice are having a three-legged race on John's back!"

"They're also racing in places that I don't want to discuss," John answered. Everyone laughed, even the rebels, who seemed to have somehow avoided the scourge and had backed into a corner of the barn to avoid any close contact with me, my fellow Americans, and our itchy visitors.

In a few minutes, when we'd done our best to clean our bodies and our clothes, we again dressed and set out on the day's march, but there were frequent hushed exclamations and much slapping of bodies as more lice came out of hiding. The guerillas kept their distance and signaled us to walk behind them. They were not taking any chances.

We marched for hours, and in the afternoon, we came to a small valley.

Ahead of us, a mountain towered steep and high; it seemed to have a wide trail going up its face. At the foot of the mountain lay a small village. We headed there and were welcomed by. approximately forty people, which was a higher population than the previous villages. The inhabitants were all grown men and women. There were no children playing, no babies in the arms of the women.

The people kindly offered us polenta and water, and an unusual treat, a small piece of ham for each of us. We were moved by the generosity of the rebels and their sup porters, sharing with us the little food that they had.

When we finished our meager but much appreciated meal, the rebels led us through the village. Just past the village we came out into an open space and saw, sitting upon a narrow gauge railroad track, an old railroad engine with several cars connected behind it. Some were open, gondola-style cars, and others were closed boxcars. The train track led from the village up the side of the mountain. The American crewmen all looked at one another, not sure whether to be amused or afraid. The old steam engine looked very old and well worn!

The rebels and more than a dozen villagers climbed into the open cars and signaled for us to board one of the boxcars.

"Nijedan dozvola!" ("No lice!"), one of the villagers explained, pointing to our itchy bodies and laughing.

Our boxcar did not have doors, so we sat in the open doorways on each side of the car, our feet hanging out into space as the engine chugged laboriously up the mountain as the valley and brown-roofed homes of the village shrank below us. The sun was hot, but a breeze stirred our hair and cooled our skin as the train slowly climbed up the slope. We began to relax, enjoying the luxury of the ride. Some men closed their eyes, faces lifted to the sun and cool air. Some distractedly picked lice off their clothes while their eyes took in the broad expanse of mountainsides embroidered with patches of green trees.

I watched the landscape chug past the door through half-closed eyes. Fred was sitting next to me.

"Be nice if we could ride this a few hundred miles," I said to him.

He stuck his head out the door, craning his neck to see the track ahead of us, then looked doubtful and chuckled, "We'll be lucky if it gets us to the top of the mountain." I smiled in agreement. However, when I looked at the railroad track running beneath my feet, my amusement was replaced with real concern: there were frequent repair patches where the Germans had once bombed out the track. The repairs looked makeshift, and did not inspire my confidence. I pulled my feet in and held onto the side of the car. Fred grinned at me.

We had been on the train for about a half hour, and

we were nearing the top of the mountain. The view was spectacular: mountains marched into the distance, range after range. Green valleys in the deep gorges hinted of ease and spring. Gracious trees covered the lower slopes in green sterling trim. I began to relax again. The chug, chug, chugging of the train had lulled me into a drowsy, dreamy state.

Suddenly, the sound of the train changed: it was laboring with great bellows and growls and was slowing down. The locomotive pulled, and the train gained a few yards. A blast of smoke and a roar from the engine, and it gained a few yards more, but still it slowed. With a screech and a hiss, the engine gave a final, desperate tug, and then it stopped. For a moment, we stood still: the train and all the people on it. Then the train began to inch backward, slowly at first, then faster.

"The engine's failed! Everyone hold on!" Fred yelled.

The members of the Maggie's Drawers crew lunged into the corners of the boxcar, grasping for handholds on the smooth, wooden walls. There was a loud squeal as the operator applied the train's brakes. The cars lurched in a stop and go motion as the brakes held and then let loose, held and let loose. We were still going way too fast, and visions of the makeshift track repairs filled my head – along with visions of the train rolling down the mountain, smashing into pieces on the sharp rocks.

My fingernails scraped along the walls as I tried to hold myself in place. The other men were also struggling to brace themselves against the floor and sides of the car, eyes wide with concern, as the car continued to lurch and the squealing of the brakes was joined with the smell of hot metal. I was slowly being jerked toward the door, my feet planted against the wooden floorboards, my arms dragging along the wooden wall. Every time the train lurched and slowed, I'd push myself toward the back of the car, but when the brakes failed and the train lunged forward again, I'd be hurled toward the center of the car, and toward the door as the car swayed wildly back and forth.

I was losing ground and feared that at any moment I'd be flung out of the boxcar and slammed into the rocks along the tracks.

"Grab my hand!" It was Fred, stretching out his hand toward me, his other holding tightly to a metal knob of some sort on the wall. I flipped on my stomach and stretched out my hand toward his. The train lurched and I slid farther away. The train paused, and I lunged toward his hand; the train lurched forward, I fell flat on my stomach again. I inched my way forward, hand outstretched, and just as my fingertips touched Fred's, the motion of the train smoothed out and slowed down. The operator had gained control of the train's slide. We were now easing much more slowly down the mountain.

Fred grasped my hand and pulled me into a sitting position next to him. I sighed with relief as the rest of the men relaxed and sprawled on the boxcar floor.

"That would have been a hell of a way to go," said Reilly.

"Guess we should have packed parachutes," said Clarence.

Everyone laughed.

But our laughter was short-lived as the roar of an airplane engine hit our ears. We heard the plane overhead and a nearby explosion deafened us. It came from the front of the train.

I peeked out the door. A German fighter was circling; it had spied the train and was planning its attack. It had already dropped a bomb that had destroyed the railroad tracks in front of the train.

The pilot made a broad turn and swept toward us, coming in low, firing his guns. The bullets peppered the ground in a path leading up to the train, and as we flung ourselves down onto the floor, we heard them striking the tram.

There was the sound of machine gun fire from one of the gondolas as the rebels shot at the attacker. The German fighter flew away from the threat of ground fire.

The train reached the bottom of the mountain, and was gliding across an open space toward the village where we started.

"Hold on!" someone shouted.

The train came to an abrupt halt as it hit a pile of dirt at the end of the railroad tracks.

As we emptied the boxcar, jumping lightly to the ground, we saw the rebels swing down from their car; their faces were full of fury as they ran up to the train operators, screaming and pointing alternately at the engine then the pile of firewood.

Though we could not understand their exact words, we figured out that the operators had failed to take along enough fuel to get the train to the top of the mountain.

Two of the villagers who were on the train had been shot in the fighter's attack; they had blood on their feet and arms. None of our crew was injured.

One of the rebels pointed up to the tracks. There was a gap in the rail where the German fighter had dam aged it. There would be no second try.

"Mozemo ici ovuda," ("We must go this way") a rebel said, pointing to a faint trail on the side of the mountain.

After a brief rest, we followed the rebels up the trail toward the mountaintop.

"You know, suddenly, walking doesn't seem so bad," Fred said with a smile.

The rest of us had to agree as we began our trudge up the mountain.

The sun had become an enormous orange wheel as it sank into the west.

Shortly after nightfall we stopped. I laid down to rest.

Rings On My Cane

Bill's cane made during the escape route. The rings carved on it indicate the days on the ground.

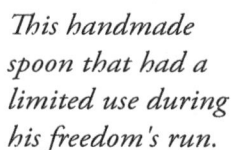

This handmade spoon that had a limited use during his freedom's run.

CHAPTER 11

Reflections

While resting, I began to think about the train, and remembering my childhood, when one of my chores was to scour the railroad tracks for small lumps of coal that had fallen from the trains. Sometimes, I had to walk seven or eight miles down the tracks to collect just one pail of coal. The coal was used to fire up the old iron range Grandma used to cook our meals.

Having a little coal was crucial to survival.

This was after my mother and Frank were thrown out of the stone house for not paying the rent. We moved in with my mother's father, his wife, and their two young daughters.

Granddad was a carpenter by trade. We all lived in a ramshackle house on an unworkable farm in the sand dunes next to the railroad tracks, miles from the nearest neighbor.

The girls and I amused ourselves by pumping pails full of water and pouring them into gopher holes, trying to drown the rodents out of their holes. The gophers were everywhere, by the hundreds. In spite of our efforts, we never drowned one out of his hole. The sandy soil just absorbed the water.

One day, Grandfather came home saying that he had rented a house in Dutton.

"Where is Dutton?" I asked my mother. "It's not that far away," she answered.

"Is it closer to my brother, Harold?" I asked. She did not answer.

Once again, everything was thrown into the car, and we were off on another exodus.

My Grandfather, with his family, moved to a clap board house and we moved into one like it next door. This meant another new school for me. I had to adjust to being the new kid on the block, an experience that I had had the chance to practice several times already.

The year was 1927. I watched my grandmother making home-brew beer in 20 gallon crocks.

"It is under doctor's advice," she said to me. "It will be good for your Aunt Josephine, who has the St. Vitus Dance disease."

Aunt Josephine was Grandfather's daughter and my mother's younger, half sister. I didn't know if Grandmother was telling me the truth. But I knew that the brew seemed to be good for her and the other folks she sold it to, because it seemed to make everyone happy.

I wet my lips with my tongue. A few swallows of that brew would make me happy now.

One night carloads of police and revenue officers surrounded our makeshift houses. Tough-looking officers searched our homes and found Grandmother's home-brew operation. The brewing crock was the first thing to go, smashed into hundreds of pieces.

Grandmother, a feisty specimen, stood in the middle of the tough men, yelling at them. "This beer is a prescription for Josephine!" she protested over and over.

The officers ignored her. They loaded the full bottles of brew into their cars.

But Grandmother was not easily daunted. When an officer picked up her hand-operated bottle capper, she grabbed it away from him, her eyes glaring in unspoken challenge. Facing a mad, three hundred pound Grandma, the officer gave up.

Finally, Grandmother convinced the officers to call the doctor, who confirmed what Grandmother was saying. I remember the doctor as a man who took a real interest in the well-being of his patients because he visited quite frequently to sample his "prescription," and to ensure that it was just right for my aunt.

However, the officers were unimpressed with the doctor's "prescription." They shrugged their shoulders and left, taking the full bottles of beer, not paying any attention to Grandmother, who was calling them thieves and thugs for taking the prescription brew.

Grandmother's were not the only bootlegging entrepreneurial activities in the family: Frank was buying uncut moonshine and selling watered down whiskey. He added about three gallons of water to every gallon of uncut moonshine to yield about four gallons of "whiskey." He funneled his mix into pint and quart medicine bottles. Each bottle had ounce markings on the glass so that "patients" could tell exactly how much medicine they were taking.

Frank had hidden his whiskey jugs in the weeds along the fence-row about three hundred feet back from our house. While the officers searched the homes, they did not look along the fencerow, so Frank saved his whiskey.

In a way, this was good news, because he would make enough money to pay the rent so we could stay in the clapboard house a while longer. Shortly after this episode, Grandpa, Grandma, and the girls moved to Grand Rapids. I was very sad to see them go.

A couple of weeks later, I arrived home from school to find no one home. I figured that Frank and my mother had gone somewhere. So much the better, I enjoyed being alone. But the police officer arrived at our door and told me to come with him.

Riding in the police car, I wondered what was happenmg.

"Did Mother and Frank get into an accident?" I thought. "I hope they are okay."

The officer took me to the police station and asked me to sit on the bench and wait.

I sat in quiet confusion, surrounded by loud mouthed characters arguing with the police.

I was surprised to see my father walk in. With no

The Last Mission

explanation, he guided me to his car. We drove out to the clapboard house with a police car following. Dad and I went into the house and we picked up my meager belongings; then he drove me to my Aunt Stella's home in Lansing.

During the entire trip, my father did not say a word about Frank and Mother.

Aunt Stella was one of Dad's older sisters. She and Father had a heated argument. "Let me adopt the boy, Harvey," I heard my aunt saying.

"No way, he's my son, I'll take care of him," Father answered.

I sat patiently as people decided my future. Finally, Father left, telling me that he would be back soon.

My Aunt Stella and her husband, Albert, had a nice home. They owned a tailor shop and the business provided a good life for them. But for me, it meant another school, and another group of kids.

Still, I had no idea where Mother and Frank were at the time.

I lived with my aunt long enough to survive the measles, and I guess that was just about enough for Aunt Stella, too.

I really don't know why I left Aunt Stella's house.

All I know is that Father came to pick me up one day.

That is when I found out that my father was a fish monger, selling fish from house to house out of his small Model T pickup truck, which he had filled with ice and fish.

Reflections

My father drove me to a stranger's house, saying that I would be boarding there for a while. The people boarding me were Mr. and Mrs. Roberts. They had a son named Joseph who was two years older than I and had no time for a little kid like me. After school, I was on my own, and I had to find ways to amuse myself. I seldom saw or heard from my father. I missed my brother, Harold.

After my parents had divorced, my father had taken Harold to his brother's farm. Uncle John, and his wife, Clella, had no children of their own. They had agreed to keep Harold for a few weeks until Dad got back on his feet. The few weeks became months because, apparently,

Father had a difficult time getting back on his feet.

One day that summer, as I was roaming the boarding house, bored and lonely, I saw my father's Model T drive up out front. I ran to the front door and rushed outside. As the screen door slammed behind me, the passenger door on the truck opened. A tall, thin young man stepped out. It was my brother, Harold.

We were elated to see each other, and we talked for hours and hours. Finally, Harold broke the news to me that Frank and Mother were in jail. I was mad that my father had not told me earlier. That was the first time that I understood my father's weakness. He brought Harold to tell me about Mother and Frank.

The rays of the morning sun sprayed over the mountains of Yugoslavia, warming my face and turning the inside of my eyelids red. It was time to move on, on toward the top of another mountain. I carved another ring on my cane, picked a few lice from my clothes, and with the others, began the ascent. It was early afternoon when we reached the top of the mountain.

Baby Billy with brother Harold and Mother and Father

Reflections

*1. Approximate location when shot down
*2. Approximate location of the secret airfield
*3. Bari, Italy, was the final desination of freedom

CHAPTER 12

The Highest Mountain

There was an entire village on top of the mountain. Most of the buildings were in ruins, destroyed by German bombs, but a few homes still stood, etched on the sides of the mountain. They had survived the bombings because of their sheltered position.

There was an unusual amount of activity in the village, much more than we had seen in previous villages. There were a few stores open, a general store with very little merchandise on display, a barbershop and a coffee house. There were other storefronts, but they were all abandoned and most were in ruins. In the streets of this village, I saw a rare mechanical mode of transportation. It was a strange looking invention, an automobile, like a Model T Ford, but it had a large upright boiler sitting on a platform sticking out of the rear of the car. The platform was loaded with wood. From time to time, the driver would get out and fill up the boiler with the wood; the vehicle could only go a few miles before it was time to throw more in. It was an ingenious innovation in response to the German confiscation of gasoline.

Our rebel guides stopped by the roadside coffeehouse. On the outside, under a huge pine tree, there were a few round, iron tables and several wooden chairs with straw seats. On one of those chairs sat a beautiful woman. She had long, black, wavy hair and deep, mysterious brown eyes. "Maria Italiana," one of the rebels said, pointing at her.

Another woman came running out of the coffee house. She spoke to the rebels with great agitation in her voice. She was pointing ahead down a dirt road.

The rebels motioned for us to sit down. "Sjedni, sjedni," "Sit, sit," they said as they took off running in the direction the irate woman pointed.

The Italian woman smiled. "Hello, I am Maria."

We introduced ourselves. She spoke quite a few words of English, enough for us to understand that she was looking for a way out of Yugoslavia and that she was going to join our group walking to the promised land.

With some English and broken Italian, we managed to ask her if she knew where we were.

"Come here," she said, and she entered the coffee house.

The woman behind the counter started talking loudly to us, waving her hands. A few old wooden tables and chairs were standing on the wooden floor. Maria guided us to one of the whitewashed walls where a map was nailed up.

The woman stopped talking, finally realizing that none of us understood what she was saying.

Maria pointed with her finger to the map.

The Last Mission

"Ecco," ("Here,") she said.

She was pointing to the heart of Yugoslavia. It was difficult to know the exact location because the map was written in Yugoslavian. But calling on my sketchy geographical knowledge of the country, I figured she was pointing to the border between Serbia and Bosnia.

"We are entering Serbian territory," Fred confirmed. He must have made better grades in geography than some of us.

Maria's finger traveled up the map. It stopped at the highest point of Yugoslavia, close to the Austrian border. "Penso che lei cada qui," ("I think you fall here,") she said.

"That is where our plane went down," Fred remarked. "That must be the territory where we bailed out. We have walked through Slovenia, Croatia, and part of Bosnia," Fred continued, and he ran his finger in a straight line from the top of Yugoslavia to the place we were now. "Dobbiamo andare giu qui," ("We must go down here,") Maria said, pointing farther down. "Montenegro!!" several men exclaimed, their dismay evident.

"Well, at least we are halfway there," I said as I placed my finger next to Fred's and drew it down the map from our current location to Montenegro. I began to understand that we were headed south so we would be directly across the Adriatic Sea from Lecce, Italy, when we were lifted to safety. The aircraft would have a short flight, increasing the odds for a safe trip.

The aircraft that were used to rescue surv1vmg

- 99 -

servicemen were not in any way equipped for combat. In any air-to-air engagement with the enemy, there would be absolutely no chance of survival.

I looked at the map. We had walked a long way to get here, and we had a long way to go.

Loud voices sounded from outside of the coffee house.

We stepped outside and saw that our leaders, the ones who had run down the road, were back, bringing with them two men whose hands were tied behind their backs. The four of them argued passionately. The woman from the coffeehouse pointed to the two men with their hands tied behind their backs.

"To su oni! To su oni!" ("That's them! That's them!") she yelled again and again.

The rebels yelled at the two men, pointing their fingers in their faces as if they were lecturing them. The tied men shook their heads, "No, No," they said with terror in their eyes. The only word I understood was "Mihailovic." "No, No," the captured men repeated. But they were not convincing enough. One of our leaders grabbed the hair of one of the captured men and pulled his head back. With a quick move, before anyone understood what was coming, he pulled a long knife from his waist and sliced the throat of the screaming man. His blood splattered several feet away. The man's body jerked a few times and then as he fell to the ground with blood pouring out of his neck.

The other man began to shake like a leaf in the wind,

pleading for his life. His cries did not move the rebels, and his throat was sliced with the same knife.

A couple of feet away, there was a ditch, where the first lifeless body was thrown. The other body was kicked into the ditch next to his friend.

An uneasy feeling stirred in my stomach. The dead men were Mihailovic's people who had stopped by the coffeehouse for a drink. The lady proprietor had overheard them planning to inform the Germans where Tito's Partisans, and the Americans, were going to pass through German lines that night. Maria explained this to us as best she could.

The Germans would pay good money in exchange for information that would lead to the capture or death of Tito's Partisans. They would pay even more for information about Allied airmen.

Fighting the Partisans in the mountains was a difficult task. It was easier to ambush them in the valleys at night.

The two Mihailovic men had received a different reward than they had expected.

Soon, we were ready to go on our way. We jumped over the ditch in which the bodies were lying.

Maria walked with us. She had good energy and tried to keep everyone's spirits high by joking and singing Italian songs. She tried to get us to sing along, but we were not in the mood.

That night, we had to pass through a fairly large German-occupied city in the valley. Our journey was becoming more dangerous with every step. We were caught between the Germans and Mihailovic's Chetniks.

There was not much left of the city. Homes were destroyed and storefronts closed, either by fallen debris or heavy steel shutters. With the moon's brightness to guide us, we passed through the city, moving very quietly around the German camp.

At the far edge of the city, we came to a bridge about twenty feet long. A German soldier guarded each end of the bridge.

The Partisans who were leading signaled us to sit and wait. We were at the foot of a small hill that was covered with trees. We watched four rebels fade into the darkness around the bridge. Like phantoms, they climbed under the structure, two of them crossing to the other side. There was one German on each side, and it was an easy task for the Partisans to take them out quietly.

One of the Partisans came back and signaled us to move east. We stepped onto the bridge, passing the body of the first German soldier. We ran across quickly and quietly, stepping over the body of the second German soldier at the other end. Some of the Partisans were busy installing explosives under the bridge. As soon as we saw their intent we were off running for the nearest mountain.

We were about 100 yards away when a tremendous explosion deafened my ears. I glanced behind me. The air was filled with fireworks.

"Bjezi! Bjezi!" ("Run! Run!") the Partisans urged, and we did, as fast as we could.

The Last Mission

To Sgt William M. Kollor
ASN 36175843
98TH Bomb. Group (H)
415TH Bomb Squadron (H)
A.P.O. 520 % Postmaster
New York, New York

From Mr. Mrs. Dave Woodwyk
806 So. Division Ave
Lowell Michigan
March 14, 1944

Dear Bill:

Just a few lines letting you know I am still thinking of you. It has been so long from us. Hoping this letter finds you in 100 per cent of health. Bill you wrote about me going trucking. I sure would like to. You said you would furnish $200. for a truck if I can do this I would have you with me after the war is over which would you rather do trucking on the road or would you sooner have Del Krops moving outfit. Why I am asking you this Bill if I go thru I will have it on our names together if you want to do this you can send the money if you think this alright if I can't get a truck right off I will put it in the Bank for safe keeping till I get a truck. Well Bill let me know if it is all right to you or not. Well Bill we are all feeling fairly Good but Ray isn't so hot. Well Bill keep your chin up and keep up hopes and pray to God to see you back think you soon. It will be sooner.

Dave Woodwyk
Lowell Michigan

— 103 —

The Highest Mountain

CHAPTER 13

Death in the Valley

*F*or the next two days, we walked and rested, stopping in little villages for a plate of polenta, on our way to the promised land.

Maria displayed great stamina keeping up with the pace of the team. At least now, there was someone who could speak some English, and some Yugoslavian, and be a bridge of communication between the Americans and the Partisans.

In one of the villages, we picked up a British major. He was tall and thin, and wore a patch over his left eye, an eye he'd obviously lost in a battle. He clarified our situation when he told us, "We should reach our destination in about ten days."

The major was in British Intelligence and had parachuted into Yugoslavia a few months before. "I am sick to death of this place, lads," he said. He would not tell us his name. "Call me Major," he said. The day after we picked up the major, we reached a small valley that was under cultivation. It had been freshly plowed.

"They'll be putting in the corn and wheat soon," the major explained.

"Oh great, more polenta," I said.

"Look, they must plant crops that grow quickly, those poor blokes are hungry now," he explained.

The valley was about a mile long and a half mile wide; it was enclosed by a horseshoe shaped string of mountains. A canyon lay at the open end of the mountains. Pine trees adorned the slopes, and a crystal clear stream flowed from the top of the horseshoe down the side of the valley and into the canyon.

It was late afternoon when we reached the valley. We entered it from the canyon side. The canyon was about 300 feet deep. Through the thick foliage of the trees that had sprouted throughout the canyon, I could see the stream of water that ran to the bottom. I stood for a moment to marvel at the beauty around me. The only sounds were the rolling of the water and the singing of a few brave birds.

The air stood still and thin, the sun was about to set. Vivid orange stripes were brushed across the blue sky. The mellow sunlight framed the multitude of pine trees, the valley, and the green canyon in a peaceful embrace; a picture drawn by the hand of God.

We walked alongside the creek up into the valley. A small village was nestled at the foot of the mountain. Its rooftops were nested among trees. There was a lot of activity in the village. It was one of the few times that I had seen children, and there was also more livestock than in the other villages.

Our leader pointed us to the houses whose inhabitants had agreed to give us something to eat. By now, I was swimming in my clothes, I had lost so much weight.

The elderly woman who lived in the house welcomed me in and fried an egg for me. She served it on a plate with polenta.

I was curious about polenta, which had sustained me for so many days, and I later asked how it was made. I was told that it consisted mainly of ground corn, with a little oat straw added for filler. The mixture was boiled in water until it was the consistency of oatmeal.

"Thank you," I said to the woman. She bowed her head and smiled.

She had fried the egg on a big rock on the floor that was her stove. There was a hole in the ceiling for the smoke to go out.

No matter how it was cooked, the egg looked good on the plate. I pulled my wooden spoon from my pocket and slowly ate my meal. The enticing aroma of baked bread broke into my nostrils. I looked over to the cooking area, and saw an inverted cup-shaped pan full of bread. There were hot coals packed around it. The woman lifted the pan from the coals with tongs. She freed the bread onto a towel and brought it to me. I picked up the small loaf of bread, thanked her sincerely, and went out to share my bounty with my friends.

After we ate, we walked back down to the other end of the valley to a small shed. That was a safe place to take a nap.

I suddenly realized I could hear gunfire raging on the far horizons beyond the mountains.

From the British major and Maria, I learned that

there was a vicious battle between the Germans and the Partisans in the valley beyond the U-shaped mountains, the same valley that we were supposed to pass through sometime during the night. The Germans were trying to take the mountains, and the Partisans were defending them.

An uneasy feeling settled in my body. I did not want to be sleeping if the Germans came through. The British major saw my anxiety. "You needn't be too worried," he said. "The Germans have been looking to take this mountain for the better part of four years."

That explained the children and the plethora of live stock in the village; the residents felt secure.

We slept in the shed until midnight. Then we went back to the village where our guides were waiting and we began the steep climb up the slope of the mountains at the far end of the valley.

The biting air of the cloudy night urged us to walk fast in order to keep warm. We reached the top of the mountain and started down the other side. We were to enter the German-held valley by 3:00 a.m.

The darkness concealed a mystery as our shadows moved through the trees that towered high. Occasional gunfire came from the valley ahead and broke the stillness of the night. Suddenly, I felt the hand of one of our guides pushing me behind a tree and he whispered something. Everyone in our group disappeared behind tree trunks.

I could see two shadows coming up the mountain. I held my breath. Then our guides stepped out and began to talk to them in low voices.

It was then that I realized the two men were Partisans. They began an animated dialogue with our guides, pointing toward the valley and then toward the top of the mountain. Our guides seemed to be urging the two new comers to go back the way they had come.

Later I would learn that the battle was still raging down in the valley. The rivals had attacked one another in a bloody chaos.

The men rolled around in the bloody grass as they savagely slit each other's throats, and they tore each other's bellies. The clash among men lacerated the night. The uproar of men slaughtering each other was for a few inches of land.

And killing, that most ancient need of man, took on a high mystical meaning. Throughout the night there was flesh against flesh.

Our group turned away from these unseen terrors and made our way back over the mountain to the village we had left only hours before. We were told to go back to the shed and rest; we would try again to cross the next valley tomorrow night. I was exhausted. Using stones for my pillow, I fell asleep.

We woke about 7:00 a.m. and walked toward the village, hoping to get something to eat.

I started toward the house of the elderly lady who had fed me the day before. I hoped that she would have some bread ready.

As I walked along the front wall of the stone house

Death in the Valley

and headed for the door, machine gun fire suddenly deafened my ears. Bullets ripped the wall ahead of me. At the same time several Partisans ran by me, yelling and motioning for me to follow them. I forgot my hunger, and the fresh baked bread, and ran for my life.

By the time I reached the end of the village, all hell had broken loose.

There was machine gun fire coming from three different directions. Field mortar shells were landing all around us; the explosions were sending lethal shrapnel everywhere.

It was an unexpected turn of events. Everyone seemed to be surprised. People were running in pandemonium to the open end of the field.

The night before, the Germans had defeated the Partisans and advanced up the mountain. They had set up their machine guns, mortars and riflemen along three sides of the valley.

Then, they waited for daylight.

As the sun rose over the horizon the Germans set their aim at us and the villagers. They waited until we were all in the village.

Then they started firing.

As I reached the open valley beyond the village I felt that my chances of survival were remote.

Ahead of me unfolded a terrifying scene: women, children, and elders were frantically running toward the canyon that lay at the open end of the valley.

Horses and cattle ran along with the people among

the mortar explosions.

There was also a team of horses pulling a large buck board wagon loaded with women and children. The village men were running behind it trying to shield their women and children from this deadly force, which was overtaking them.

I had no choice. I threw myself into the rain of gun fire with the rest.

As I ran through the destruction of iron and fire, I found myself engulfed in smoke and dust and screams and anguish. I ran as fast as I could. A mortar shell exploded to my right; it landed between the horses pulling the wagon. In my peripheral vision, I saw people and horses lifted several feet into the air and blown to pieces, among them several children. Through the smoke, I saw women, now carrying children in their arms, in a frantic run to safety. Men were helping the wounded and elders trying to get away from the fire of death.

A chunk of hot metal from an explosion hit me, just above my ankle, taking a piece of meat from my leg.

A few yards ahead of me and to my left, spurts of dust from machine gun fire warned me of danger. I hit the ground. On my way down, a small piece of hot metal sheared off a part of one of my knuckles. Most of the machine gun fire was coming from my rear. The assault continued relentlessly and without mercy. Lying on the ground, I pointed my feet in the direction that most of the fire was coming from, hoping to make as small a target as possible.

A burst of bullets hit underneath my right arm.

Miraculously, I was not hit.

I lifted my head trying to spot the rest of the crew. The scene was horrifying. People and animals were falling all around me, blood splattering from their wounds. The freshly plowed soil, darkly rich and ready for seeding, was covered with bodies – some completely still, collapsed in death, others mired in pain and fear. Voices of panic and screams of pain filled the valley.

I saw Fred and George drop to the ground several yards behind me. A machine gun bullet hit next to my left ear, throwing dirt into my face. Another bullet hit under my right hand that stretched out flat ahead of me. The same burst carried on and hit Fred in the leg.

"I'm hit," yelled Fred. George got on his hands and knees to help Fred. A burst of gunfire ripped through George's body. As George was falling to the ground, I saw his hands reach for his left pocket and the photograph that was tucked inside it. George's face hit the ground with both of his hands still clutching the pocket over his heart. Another rip of machine gun fire hit Fred in the other leg.

I stood up ready to head back toward them. At that moment, nothing mattered – the bursts of machine guns, the mortar fire – nothing except getting to my friends.

But, as I stood, dazed with shock and disoriented by the crushing slaughter, I saw a man walking slowly as if he were going on a Sunday stroll. I recognized the uniform – it was the British major.

"Come along, lad," he said to me.

I looked at him in wonder. How could he be so calm

amidst this destruction and death?

"I have to go back to my friends!" I yelled.

"Back that way, will only get you killed," he replied.

I tore my attention away from this calm apparition and took one step toward Fred and George. The major grabbed my arm." Pay attention, man. It's no good. Your friends are severely wounded. Even if you got them out, there's no medicine. They've better odds of survival with the Germans."

He was standing amid the carnage as if nothing was happening, carrying on an urgent but subdued conversation. But I was beyond reason; wildly, my eyes searched his face as I worked to discern his words and their meaning. Giving up, I turned away, and leaned into the wind, poised to run back to them. But the major held my arm tight and said," Once again, man, the Germans will take care of your friends. You can't be charging over there, it'll mean your death. Surely you can comprehend that!"

I looked at his face. Who was this one-eyed man with the black patch over his other eye who was telling me what to do? I saw the determination on his face that told me he was not about to let me go.

"Right, then. Stay close, don't run, and ignore the shelling. Just keep walking. If the gunners can't see any spurts of dust from where they are, they won't know how close the bullets are landing, and they'll soon find other targets."

We walked for about half a mile under machine gun fire from three directions. It seemed surreal to be walking as though we were on a stroll in the park. Yet, just as the major had said, eventually the sound of gunshots was behind us. We had escaped the slaughter and were too far away for their firing to be effective.

The clear waters of the creek running swiftly next to me were now stained red from the flowing blood.

Walking, we reached the end of the valley, went around a curve, then ran until we dropped from exhaustion. By now, the major and I had put over five miles between the Germans and us, all uphill. The machine gun sounds, the explosions, the screaming people, the blood running in the creek, these images filled my mind as if it were all a dream, yet I knew otherwise. I cut off a piece of cloth from my heated suit and wrapped it around my wounded leg.

The sun had arrived to scorch the bloodstained land; its rays spilled through the tree branches, trying to lull me to sleep.

I laid down and sleep began to take over my senses. There would be a moment of rest before the threat of death again fell upon the harsh lives of the people who had grown weary of battles, immune to death.

The people who had survived the butchering were now on the run, moving to find a safer land, leaving behind the trees in their courtyards, the songbirds in their cages, the flower pots on their windowsills, the basil and the roses in their gardens.

People had become hard and inhospitable, letting the hate simmer inside of them, mute and unrevealed hate that someday would burst out, insolent and free.

CHAPTER 14

In No Man's Land

Voices disturbed my sleep. I jolted, alert, and ready to defend myself. I was still anxious from the massacre in the valley. I relaxed as I saw it was Maria and Clarence.

They both looked exhausted, but relieved to find familiar faces.

"We were lost, wandering around trying to find the rest of our crew," Clarence said.

To my right, the British major was lying on his back, staring at the sky. I hoped that he knew where to go from here. "You chaps oughtn't to be mucking aimlessly about, out there," the major chided. "This territory is the cross roads of Partisans and Chetniks." Then he stood up and warned," One can not be certain whom one might encounter."

Maria glanced at me, rolling her eyes in mild exasperation.

My temples were hurting, throbbing, and my nerves were tense. The traumatic experience of losing George and the uncertainty of Fred's fate had discouraged me. "What is the use of carrying on?" I thought. Maria's spirit and humor briefly eased my aching mind.

The major and Maria began a conversation in Italian. He was talking, pointing over the mountain, and she was moving her hands faster than her lips. I guessed that Europeans talked a lot with their hands. It was from their hand and body language that I was able to decipher the conversation; I could tell that they could not decide which way to go.

"We will move south," the major finally said, pointing to the top of the mountain.

Another afternoon of climbing began, the most difficult so far, because my heart was heavy and my steps were slowly taking me away from Fred and George.

We reached the top of the mountain in darkness. The moon was bright that night and we continued downward on our well-lit path. We had been walking for a few more hours when we came to a place where the mountain became treacherously steep. Clouds now covered the moon. Darkness made our way even more dangerous. The decision was made to stop and rest.

It was past midnight, less than a day after the massacre in the valley we had left behind. But the scenes of what had happened there – the screams, the explosions – continued to haunt me.

My thoughts drifted to George. I wondered if he would get a proper burial. I thought of the picture that he had in his pocket, and wondered if it was now stained with blood. His wife, and the child he left behind; how would they cope with the loss, how would they survive?

I thought of Fred. Was he still alive? Had the Ger

mans taken him to a hospital and amputated his legs? Or did they shoot him on the spot, thinking him an inconvenience to carry around?

In the early morning chill, the humidity had settled on the grass blades and the tops of the trees, and made the atmosphere unusually cold. I crawled behind a large rock, seeking warmth. I had to stop thinking about all of this. I prayed to God for mercy, for sleep, for rest.

My mind drifted to the natives. They moved from village to village and mountain to mountain. Longing to see a bit of rich free soil, a friendly smile, they were uprooted from family, from home. Slowly my mind and I surrendered to exhaustion.

I saw images of tall bearded men with bandoliers and long rifles. With rage painted on their faces they climbed the rocks like wild goats and were closing in on our group.

We were sleeping peacefully, unaware of the danger. Barrels of guns were pointed at us.

Lightning fire came from the rifles. The deafening sound startled me.

I leapt up from my sleep.

I looked around trying to catch my breath. There was no one, there was nothing.

In the still of the darkness I heard the sound of running, rolling water, coming from the foot of the mountain. "Water," I thought. "That explains the unusual moisture in the air."

The people around me slept peacefully. Another day

was about to dawn.

By the time my friends woke up, I had carved another ring on my cane. The sun appeared in the east as we began our walk down the steep hill.

"I can hear and smell water running," the English major said.

Clarence and I looked at each other, thinking the same thing, but Maria said it out loud. "The British, they know everything," she said shrugging her shoulders as she headed downhill.

After about an hour's walk, we came to a steep boulder strewn slope leading down to a river. Farther down the river there was a cliff formed from solid rock hanging over the water. A path ran beneath the cliff and along the river's edge.

The clear water descended from the high mountains and rolled through the hills, and then it dropped into the deep gorge and disappeared around the mountains toward the lowlands.

Across from where we were standing, another mountain towered majestically. Trees and plants grew near the water, and the greenery spread up to the mountain slopes.

It was a spectacular view. I sat on a rock to marvel at the beauty of the earth.

"Beautiful," Maria said.

I looked at this Italian woman with admiration. She was in a land ruled by men and surrounded by death. She was determined to tackle the impossible task of survival.

"Why are you here?" I asked her.

"I came here to help the cause, to help the Partisans keep the Germans away from their villages on the mountains, and to defeat the Chetniks. I have been here in Yugoslavia for two years now. I have mostly transported food and ammunition in backpacks to the men fighting the Germans."

Maria seemed strong-minded, determined to follow her beliefs; she was involved in a war that she could have very easily avoided.

The major helped us by translating our conversation.

"And now you want to go back to Italy?" I asked.

"Yes, I must go back to Italy and to my son who needs me. My mother is getting too old to care for him."

The major interrupted our conversation to tell us that it was time to cross the river.

Getting to the water's edge down the steep mountainside was, at best, challenging. We had to hold onto different plants, trees, and at times, each other, relying on their strength for safety.

There were times when one of us lost his balance and we found ourselves sliding down the mountainside for several yards. As we regained our balance we were able to catch our breath, ending up with no more damage than a couple of skinned knees and a racing heart.

After the adventurous downhill trek, we reached the river's edge.

The crystal clear water looked inviting. The warm,

bright noonday sun shone high over our heads. We looked at each other and smiled. "Why not?" I said as we joyfully walked into the water, clothes and all. The water was icy cold, but it felt wonderfully refreshing. We were able to wash off some of the grime and dirt from the journey for the first time since leaving the base in Lecce.

My body was just getting adjusted to the icy cold water when the major insisted that we had to move on.

"We must get to the other side of this river," he said.

And so we began our fifty-yard walk through the rushing water.

The river was not deep. At first, we were thigh high in the water, and as we reached the middle of the river it was only waist deep, but the current was swift and strong. We had difficulty staying on our feet. We tried to keep moving, holding on to one another for support. But it was impossible to move. The power of the water kept pushing us back. It was as though my legs were paralyzed.

We gave up the idea of crossing the river and returned to shore, climbing back up the slope we had slid down only an hour ago.

We found a big boulder and sat behind it, to dry out and try to figure out where to go from there. After a short discussion, we decided to follow the river path and try to find a fjord or a bridge to help us get across.

Suddenly, we heard voices. Maria placed her index finger against her lips and signaled for us to keep quiet. We carefully peeked from behind the rocks and saw two men on the river path, walking downstream. They looked much like the rebels who had led us through the mountains. Their clothing was worn and ragged and they had beards and army style hats. They carried guns around their waists and over their shoulders.

"What luck," I thought with a smile. Clarence must have had the same thought because we both looked at Maria and the major, wondering why they were not standing up, asking the rebels for help.

Maria looked at us and shook her head. "No, no, no," she whispered. "Soggiorno giu," ("Stay down,") she said, signaling with her hand to stay put.

After the two men passed, she motioned to us that the men would cut our throats, saying the word "Mihailovic."

"How does she know that?" I asked Clarence.

"I have no idea," he answered with a puzzled expression on his face.

The two men walked around the bend of the river where the huge cliff hung out over the water. Passing under the cliff along the path, they went out of sight.

"Let's bide our time, gents," the major suggested.

We waited.

The water in the river running to the lowlands was the only sound that disturbed the still of the afternoon. Suddenly, gunshots rang out from the other side of the cliff, breaking the silence.

The two men came running out from under the

overhang. They were looking behind them, firing their pistols as they ran, sending a barrage of bullets toward three other men who appeared from around the bend. These men were running fearlessly against the oncoming bullets, shooting at the two men in front of them. The exchange of gunfire intensified as the two men reached below our hiding place. That was when one of the two men was hit. Several bullets stitched his body, and he screamed words I could not understand. His friend took a look at him, glanced at the three men rushing up the path, and then dove into the river. The man who was hit dropped onto his knees, screaming, dying in agony, clawing at the ground with his hands.

The three hunters spread out on the riverbank, anticipating that the man in the river would eventually come up for air. He did come up a couple of times, and he was used for target practice. A thin red strip brushed on top of the clear river water and extended around the over hang.

The three men stood over the prone man and emptied their pistols into him until they were certain that all remains of life had left his body.

Maria stood up and yelled, "Partisans, Partisans!" I was not sure she knew what she was doing. I was hoping that she was right in her assessment that the three men were Partisans.

When the three men heard the yelling, they turned around and pointed their pistols in our direction. Maria ran and slipped down the cliff. When she reached the river bank, she began talking to the men and pointing in our direction. We came out of our hiding place and followed Maria. She was right; the men were Partisans.

She spoke to them in a mixed language of Italian and Yugoslavian. Through this hybrid dialect she was able to successfully communicate with them. The men answered her and pointed down the river. I could tell from their actions that they were showing us the way across its rolling waters. Their conversation flowed, as did the blood of the dead man at their feet.

"Grazie," ("Thank you,") Maria said.

The rebels came and hugged the three of us, rattling in a foreign tongue. Then they picked up the dead body and tossed it into the river while repeating the word "Izda jice." ("Traitor.")

"One of the Partisans will come with us," Maria informed us. We proceeded under the cliff overhang and along the river path. The other two Partisans walked the opposite way, yelling, "Dobra steca, prijatelj!" 'Good luck friends' over their shoulders.

We continued down river along the path. Mountains towered on both sides of the river.

"Isn't nature magnificent?" the major commented.

My eyes took in the lush green slopes of the mountains ascending from the heart of the earth to the majestic sky, draped in wisps of white clouds. The naked and eternal beauty, the fragrance of wild flowers on this clear, windy day, made it impossible to comprehend that we were at war and that somewhere, at this very moment, this breathtaking landscape was being stained with the blood of dying people.

"Yes," I agreed.

The phrase, "no man's land", had more than one meaning here. The spirit and true beauty of this land could not be captured or possessed. It would never belong to man alone and especially not to men who would disrespect the land and seek to destroy her beauty.

We had walked for about two hours when we arrived at a point where the river narrowed. Two hills stood, one on each side of the river's banks. A bridge connected the hills. It was a swinging bridge, the same kind that I had seen in so many movies. My gut clenched a bit as I remembered the scenes in those movies. Very often, the characters were falling off of bridges like that or finding themselves clutching the ropes for dear life.

"Vedete, vedete!" ("You see, you see!") Maria pointed to the bridge.

The wind had picked up strength by now, and the bridge swayed under its power.

We had to pass over the bridge one person at a time. Clarence went first, Maria second, the major was next, then it was my turn, and the Partisan brought up the rear. The unstable bridge and the gusts of wind made the crossing difficult. I could see that some of the planks had rotted and could easily snap under my weight. I proceeded with caution, holding onto the ropes tightly and testing each wooden plank before putting my full weight on it. By. the time the bridge crossing was complete the sun was finding its way behind the mountains.

Maria and the major began another animated discussion. On occasion, they would turn to the rebel and ask him questions, but he seemed to be more confused than helpful. The major turned to us and said, "The Partisans informed Maria that beyond the mountain is a valley, heavily guarded by the Germans."

We decided that the safest thing to do would be to find a secluded spot to camp and wait for midnight to try to cross the valley. We found such a spot a short distance from the bridge and lay down to rest. Another adventurous day had passed. More deaths, more painful walking, more uncertainty and misery were now behind us.

I was unable to close my eyes and sleep. I started to pick and pick and pick lice off of my clothes. They were the only certainty for now.

Slowly my eyes began to close and I surrendered myself to this "no man's land."

CHAPTER 15

Confusing Times

I woke to the sounds of the roaring river. It felt like I had been sleeping for only a short time. The sky had turned black. The wind had picked up strength. The air swept violently from the south and pushed waves high against the riverbanks.

I curled my body up against the rocks trying to keep warm, wondering what the next day would bring. I thought about the rest of the crew and hoped that they were all alive and well, and that we would reunite with them soon. I thought of the many characters that I had met since the beginning of this adventure, the men who had saved my life and the men who had tried to take my life. I thought about the people who had become such a big part of my life, the ones who were with me now: the British major, Maria, and Clarence. How long would we be together? Who would come into my life next?

Thoughts and questions filled my mind, overwhelming me as I lay on the ground that night, lost in a land of unfamiliar sounds and traditions. My mind traveled back in time, seeking a place of familiarity.

A smile gradually spread across my face as my mind

Confusing Times

became absorbed in my childhood. There were many characters in my life back then as well, as I moved from home to home. And although those characters spoke a language that I understood and the environment was friendlier, my young mind was confused even then.

I remembered the day my father picked me up from the boarding house and took me to an old, big house in Lansing.

There, he introduced me to an older, kind lady. Her name was "Grandma See." Her two daughters lived with her along with several male boarders, including my dad and now me. One of the daughters was named Mayme Chambers, and she had two children, Evelyn and Eugene, who also lived in the big old house.

Evelyn was two years older than I was and Eugene was one year older. Eugene had red hair, so everyone called him "Red."

I often wondered how my dad knew these people, but I decided that it really did not matter.

This huge, old house suited me just fine, and the two children soon became my good friends.

I was in another new school, one of the many I had attended in my young life.

I was hesitant to make any new friends in school.

What would be the use, I'd be moving soon anyway?

Shortly after I moved into the big, old house, I found out that my father was dating Mayme Chambers.

Life was moving along routinely for a change, until

one afternoon after school. That is when my mother showed up in my life again.

Red and I were playing in the yard when a Model T Ford Coupe drove up to the house. My mother was driving the car and there was a passenger next to her. My mother got out of the car and came into the yard. I ran up to her and gave her a big hug.

I was very glad to see my mother and I was hoping that now maybe my brother would come back as well, and I could have an orderly life. It would be perfect because I liked it here. The school was good, and I had my best friend, Red, to play with.

My mother seemed happy to see me, asked how I was doing, and then spoke to my father for a while. I anxiously watched them talk, hoping that they would be able to work things out and we could have our family back together. My hopes quickly faded and then disappeared as the conversation turned into their usual arguing. My mother left saying that she had some business to take care of and that she would be back soon.

I watched her drive away with the man in the passenger seat. I found out later that the business that she had to attend to was marrying this man my mother only had met a few days ago.

The man's name was Ray Spickler.

A few days later, my mother showed up again with Ray Spickler and the Model T Ford. I had a feeling that the time had come to move again.

Confusing Times

I was right. I packed my meager belongings and climbed onto Ray's lap. Next stop was Grand Rapids. There, my mother and Ray lived in an apartment above Ray's sister's apartment. I was told to call his sister, "Aunt Dolly."

The large house owned by Aunt Dolly, was on a corner lot of a rough neighborhood.

I started attending another new school, Franklin Grade School, and since my mother had to return the borrowed Model T Ford, I had to walk about two miles each way. The school was made up of children from different ethnic backgrounds. In that school, I finally stayed long enough to make a few good friends. Two of them were black, and one of the two, Paul, became my best friend.

Paul was bigger and stronger than the other kids. He took it upon himself to protect me. I was thankful for that because there were some tough kids in that school.

I never wanted to go home because Ray was always there. He ran his business from the house and forced me to be his assistant.

He would take me by the hand and walk for several blocks, stop at a bootlegger's, and buy a gallon of uncut moonshine. Then, he would have me carry the sack with the gallon glass jug in it. He told me to drop the jug on the cement if a policeman ever stopped us. I was frightened at the thought of a policeman chasing us. I eventually figured out that Ray had me carry the jug just in case the police came, so he would be free to run away. I knew what to do

The Last Mission

if we ever got caught, but we never did.

As soon as we got home, Ray and I would go to his room and he would lock the door.

The gallon of moonshine was put into a five-gallon crock along with three gallons of water, and then enhanced with a tea-like coloring to give it that whiskey look.

When it was all mixed, we got out the pint and quart bottles. I would hold the glass funnel and Ray would fill each bottle to the full mark. Then the bottles were corked and put under the bed.

Ray would put a couple of quarts in his inside coat pocket and would give me a couple of pints to put in my coat. My mother had made me a coat with two "pint size" pockets inside for this purpose.

"If you want to go to school, you have to work,"
Ray would say.

Ray and I would saunter down the street, now and then meeting one of Ray's customers, and step into a dark niche, money and moonshine changing hands. We wanted to sell all the bottles we had with us before returning home.

My mind was mixed up. I really did not want to be out there in the dark streets with Ray, hustling whiskey. I would rather have stayed home, played, and done my homework. On the other hand, it felt good to contribute to my family and help put food on the table. "Good boy, you earned your dinner," Ray would say often.

Things were going quite well. But that was about to

Confusing Times

change. It began one fall evening.

There was a light rain and then a brisk wind. Mom, Ray, Aunt Dolly, and her husband, Uncle Bob, were playing hearts at the library table.

Next door, across the driveway, there was a party. The people at the party were extremely loud. Uncle Bob got upset, went to the bedroom, opened the window facing the house, and yelled to the neighbors to quiet down. He returned to the table and resumed playing cards. I sat by the end of the table, watching the grownups playing cards and wishing they would let me play.

Next door, the party continued to grow louder, and the profanity got heavier.

Uncle Bob got up once again, opened the window, and yelled again for them to be quiet.

There was a quiet moment, and then two shotgun blasts rang through the air.

We all ran to the bedroom. Uncle Bob was lying on the floor, his face a bloody, pulpy mess. The ambulance and police came. Of course, no one from next door knew anything about the shooting.

Uncle Bob recovered, minus an eye and an ear. Shortly after this, Uncle Bob died from a heart attack. Aunt Dolly, all alone now, needed to rent the upstairs for income, and, tired of the freeloading of her brother, she threw us out on the street.

We moved to an upstairs apartment on the south side of Grand Rapids. By this time, Ray had applied for welfare, which paid the rent and left a stipend to buy food.

I often had to wait in line at the bakery, about a half mile away from home, for the bread trucks to come back and unload their day-old bread, so I could buy it for five cents a loaf. Fresh bread cost eleven cents in the store.

And, oh yes, there was another school! School was my escape from the poverty and instability of my home. And at that new school I made a new friend, John, who was from a normal family.

John gave me a pair of his old roller skates. The problem was that the pair was missing two wheels. I made it my mission to find two wheels so I could roller-skate.

Through persistent junk pile rummaging, I was able to find another pair that had three good wheels, and I made one good pair out of the mix.

With my new wheels, I was ready to go into my new business. I partnered with another school friend, Tom, and started a magazine route. We were selling *Colliers, Liberty,* and *The Ladies Home Journal.*

I skated from one end of Grand Rapids to the other trying to sell, with not too much success.

On the day that the magazines came out, I would skate way out to Kimball's Furniture Factory; where my "real" dad now worked. I was hoping that he would buy a magazine from me, or perhaps he would give me a dime, but he never did either. I always left with a heavy heart. My own father would not even help me with my business.

Confusing Times

He simply would say "hello" and "how is school," while he went to hit the beer joints. My father had become an alcoholic at 26 years of age. As the years passed, he got worse.

Despite the disappointment of being unsupported by my father, I never gave up. I would arrive faithfully at the factory gate every time the magazines came out.

At first, there were two customers who would buy a magazine, then three, then five.

I was excited that I had five customers in the factory, but sadly, my father was never one of them. After a while, I no longer saw my father coming out of the factory door where I waited. Maybe he lost his job, or maybe he took another door. I used to tell myself that he lost his job to make myself feel better.

I kept on selling magazines to help Mother with the basic necessities, and kept hoping to see my father coming out of the factory door.

About that time, Ray's best friend, Bob, went to jail for stealing several bushels of navy beans from a farmer. Bob had poured the beans between the studding in the walls of the house he rented, to hide them.

Having formerly worked for the farmer, Bob was one of the prime suspects. When the police searched the house, they found some of the beans had leaked out from between the studding and piled up in Bob's cellar.

Bob got six months in jail and Ray let Bob's, now homeless wife, stay with us for a few months.

Our apartment had only one little, dinky bedroom where I slept in a double bed. Mom and Ray slept in another double bed in the living room. So I picked up a new bed partner, Bob's wife. At eight years old, I was sleeping with a married woman!

I was laughing to myself about that when the English accent brought me back to reality.

"Right, then, lads," the major chirped, "it's time to go."

The time had passed quickly while I was lost in the past, in my childhood.

I thought of all that I had survived back then, and I was certain that I would survive this ordeal now.

Confusing Times

1925 Model T Ford

CHAPTER 16

The Big Feast

*I*t was past midnight. The wild wind, dark skies and rolling waters were now reduced to a clear, crisp night that stretched mute and mysterious under a bright half-moon.

After our short rest stop, the group was ready to move south, to run through the German-held valley. As the five of us stood up, we noticed a dim light moving across the river.

The light flashed on and off periodically and the moonlight revealed four silhouettes moving along the opposite river bank toward the bridge. When the group reached the end of the bridge, it became obvious that they intended to cross over to our side.

"We should move out straightaway, before they cross the bridge," the major suggested.

"No, no, maybe they are friends," Maria appealed. "Cekaj, cekaj," ("Wait, wait,") our rebel guide said.

The first silhouette moved swiftly, crossing the bridge with ease. After crossing, he stopped at the foot of the bridge, about 25 feet away from our hiding place.

The next two people to cross the bridge moved at a much slower pace.

The Big Feast

The last person came across with such confidence that I knew he had made the crossing many times. When the last man stepped off the bridge, the four sat on the ground and lit cigarettes.

We heard them talking. I tried to ask Maria if they were Partisans. She did not answer. Maria turned to the rebel and whispered something to him. He seemed puzzled.

Several minutes went by. The four stood up and began to walk toward us. Silently, we tried to communicate about what would be the smart thing to do.

We decided to let them pass.

Carefully, I peeked from behind the rock where I was hiding. Their steps were growing closer. Their voices were becoming louder. I recognized two of the figures. One of them was impossible to miss because of his short, thin stature. It was Arthur "Pee-Wee" Fleming. Right behind him I saw John Reilly, the kid from Brooklyn.

At the same time, the rebel who had been hiding with us let out a sigh of relief. "Prijatelji," ("Friends,") he said. He shouted a greeting to his friends as he stood up and started walking toward them.

The rest of us came out of hiding. We exchanged handshakes and stories. I asked Arthur and John if they knew anything about the whereabouts of the rest of the crew. They had no news.

It was time to move on. Our group had now grown to nine people: there were four Americans, three Partisans, an Italian and an Englishman.

I was surprised to see that we were moving parallel to the river. This was not the way we had decided to go before the four men joined our group. The major must have seen my uncertain expression because he began to explain the change in plans to me. "Our hosts have deduced that our group has grown too large to go through the valley safely," he said. "Parts of the valley are positively brimming with land mines as well, which makes it even more perilous."

The plan was for the nine of us to circle around the valley through the woods. This way was longer, but safer. After all, we had already been walking for hundreds of miles, so a few extra steps today would make little difference to us.

The moon shone on the surface of the river. I was walking in the middle of the pack. By now, most of the pain in my groin had gone. I still kept my cane, which had become a part of me. The wooden spoon that I had carved a few days ago, was my only other possession.

One of the rebels was ahead of the pack, scouting the best way to proceed.

We walked over rocks, fallen leaves, and grass; the methodical sound of our steps kept time as the miles passed behind us. Besides our steps, the only sound came from the rolling water. No one spoke.

Another sunrise came. Another ring on my cane. We stopped on the top of a hill for a much needed rest. By now, I had become accustomed to long walks and immune to body aches. As I sat on the hilltop, I felt like I was on top of the world.

The Big Feast

The sun shone bright and warm.

If the damned lice would just go away, I would be fine.

Beneath the benevolent sun, the deep canyons, the green valleys, the tall trees, the rolling river twisting around the hills between the vivid green and the wildflowers, all created a single, harmonious impression of peaceful elegance. A soft breeze caressed my tired body. The spectacular view caused my mind to drift away from the destruction and the massacres taking place in this beautiful land.

"Time to go," someone said. And on we went once again, hiking up the inclines and descending the hills, staying close to the riverbanks.

As the sun angled to our right, its bright rays blinded our vision. This was the second day that we had gone without a meal. We stifled our hunger with edible greens that we found along the trails and quenched our thirst with water from the river.

It was late afternoon when we saw an old building by the riverbank. Its roof had caved in from enemy bombings and the only standing parts of it were some of the walls. As we approached the building I saw several airmen camped outside. We found more airmen lounging inside the building, where we tried to find ourselves a place to rest. These were airmen of the Allies, different nationalities, who had been shot down and were camping here awaiting their chance to be taken back out of Yugoslavia. This was an indicator to me that we were close to the secret valley, our gateway to the promised land, and home.

I looked around for familiar faces, but found none.

A seductive aroma filled my nostrils. It was the aroma of cooked food. I followed it down to the riverside. I had not smelled boiled food since leaving the air base in Lecce.

Several rebels were sitting around a fire. Above the fire there was a large pot hanging from a tripod. Inside the pot, an odd mixture of meats was boiling in a white broth.

The major and Maria had followed me. I stood there with a look of curiosity and obvious hunger. The rebel stirring the pot turned and looked up at us. "Tripite," ("Tripe,") he smiled, pointing to the pot. I had no idea what it was. All I knew was that I could hardly resist that smell.

"This is tripe soup," the major said. "It is made from the intestines of animals."

I was not listening. Whatever it was, my stomach was ready for it. One of the rebels stood up, picked up a bowl from the ground, and filled it with the soup.

"Svida li ti se nesto?" ("Do you like some?") he asked, extending his arm with the bowl.

I thought he would never ask. "Yes, thank you," I said.

He pulled out a hard piece of bread from a bag and handed it to me along with the bowl.

The others were also given soup and bread. I found a tree and sat in its shadow. I pulled my hand-carved spoon from my pocket, and slowly began to savor every bite of the feast. I picked every drop from my bowl. I tried

The Big Feast

to remember the best T-bone steak I had ever had; it was no match for this.

Once I had emptied the precious contents from my bowl I felt like a wolf whose hunger had been satisfied.

We spent the night in the roofless house. It was a night of welcomed rest.

In the morning, we hit the trail again. This time, we veered left of the river. My best guess was that we were moving southeast. We had three new rebels as our leaders. The rest of the team remained the same: the Englishman, the Italian, Arthur, John, Clarence, and myself.

From the top of the hill I threw a final glance behind me. The river, the greenery, the hills, befitting a postcard – I was leaving it all behind. Ahead of me lay an extensive forest. Hills and mountains sheltered the innumerable tall trees. On my far right and from a high mountaintop, a few springs released streams of water down to the woods.

There was no way a human hand could have painted such a picture.

We headed downhill. Our leaders asked us to walk directly behind them, to follow their footsteps. It was obvious that this area was full of land mines.

We were now into the dense woods. The rebel leading the pack raised his hand, signaling for us to stop. The rebels next to us pointed to the ground. We obeyed, and hit the ground, shielding ourselves behind trees. The three rebels scattered around and hid behind the thick tree trunks, positioning themselves in strategic spots.

The minutes passed in anticipation. I heard steps approaching from the right. One man appeared. He walked slowly, scouting the ground. Two more men followed a few steps behind. Our leader, who was in the front of the pack, raised his hand, signaling to his comrades to wait for his order.

I held my breath. The rest of the group sitting around me stayed still.

Two more men appeared in the back of their group. I could not see any difference between our leaders and them.

The team of five walked slowly between the trees. The man in the front was about 20 yards away.

Our leaders aimed their M-1s. The gunshots echoed through the woods, along with the yells of the ambushed Chetniks desperately calling for their comrades to take cover.

Two Chetnik rebels' bodies dropped to the ground. They were the first and the last men of the formation; one of them was crawling with great difficulty, the other was lying still – one wounded, the other dead.

The bullets coming from behind the trees crossed between the two teams of combatants.

We dug our faces into the ground, as bullets whistled over us.

The firing continued intensely for a few moments. The Chetniks were dug into their positions. One of our leaders crawled to his left, trying to find a position to fire at the enemy. Another one of our leaders pulled out a hand grenade and let it fly. After the explosion, two of the Chetniks started to retreat. One of them suddenly stopped as if his foot was glued to the ground. The other one hid behind a large rock.

One of our leaders told the rest to hold their fire. He had a smile on his face.

"I'll wager that man has stepped on a mine," the major whispered. "He dare not move or the mine will explode."

I watched the rebel destined to die. He had turned to look back, terror on his face!

Our leader, the one ahead of everyone, raised his rifle and aimed. Was this to be a merciful killing? I was hoping he would aim at the man's heart so he would die before exploding, but that was not to be. He aimed at the right foot, the one on the land mine. The impact of the bullet moved the rebel's foot. Fire and dirt erupted from the ground. There was a human cry as pieces of stones, dirt, and body parts exploded into the air.

Then there was silence.

"Ubojice!" ("Killers!") a voice said from behind the large rock. The Chetnik man who was hiding behind it stood up and began to shoot his rifle. He was frantic, shooting and yelling. He ran out of ammunition for his rifle and pulled out his revolver, and shot until it too was empty.

Our leaders waited until the man had no more ammunition, and then began to shoot at him. The frantic rebel was hit numerous times, yet he refused to drop.

"Ubojice! Ubojice!" he kept screaming, as more

bullets ripped through his body.

He finally dropped to the ground, dead.

Everyone waited until it was quiet. The hand grenade supposedly killed the fifth man. Our leaders were careful to make sure that their enemy was eliminated.

One Partisan stood beside one of the first two who has been shot, and emptied his rifle into him. Apparently, that one was still alive.

Our leaders wanted to get us moving.

A strange sensation overcame me as I was passing the dead bodies. The image of the man blown to pieces from the land mine stayed intact in my mind. This made my steps more cautious as I walked onward. The dead Chetniks brought reality to my mind. All the training and the theories about wars count for nothing when you see people's lives ending in these gruesome ways.

By sundown, we reached a small village on the slopes of a small hill, buried under the tall trees. The village seemed deserted. Some of the houses were burned and others were looted and destroyed.

"Chetniks," said one of our leaders, pointing to the burned homes.

The rebels checked the few homes for people, alive, wounded or dead. There was no one.

Our leaders conversed for a few minutes, then motioned us to follow them. We walked for about half an hour under the tall trees. The rebels were searching for something.

The Big Feast

"What are they looking for?" I asked the major, who seemed to know everything.

"I expect they're looking for dead bodies," he said. We found nothing in that direction. We turned back, passed through the deserted village, and walked the opposite way. The rebels led and we followed.

We were not far from the village when an awful stench hit my nostrils. The rebels ahead of us covered their faces with their neckerchiefs.

We walked deeper into the stench.

The rebels stopped at the edge of a deep hole, and one of them turned to us.

"Dodi ovamo!" ("Come here!") one of them motioned to us. We moved closer.

As we approached, the stench became unbearable. We covered our mouths and noses with our shirts. We reached the edge of the hole and what I saw inside is difficult to describe. Bodies of men, women, and children were piled up one on top of another. Their bodies were deteriorated; some had been partly eaten by ravens.

I turned my head.

We all turned our heads. I could not look any longer. My stomach was turning. My heart was saddened beyond expression.

In the tops of the trees, birds were flying. They were black birds of death. Their song was a monotonic sound of hunger for human flesh.

Maria held onto a tree and emptied the little food

that she had in her stomach. "Come puo la genta fare questa?" ("How can people do this?") she cried.

I walked away from the stench. My heart was bleeding with sorrow. The vision of the hole roared in my mind, nesting in my conscience. A cruelty of that kind was sim ply incomprehensible.

"Vidis. Moras reci," ("You see. You must tell,") one of the rebels kept saying.

The major and Maria tried to explain to us that we had to tell everyone about the atrocities. Even though I owed my life to the Partisans, even though what I just saw filled me with wrath, this was a war between two irregular armies. They were two teams of people who saw an opportunity to grasp a bit of power so they could promote the political agenda of their superiors. People whose children, not long ago, had played together, now were killing the sons and daughters of their countrymen. No, this was a war that did not concern me. I had to stay focused and fight my war. For this, I had to get back to my base in Lecce, Italy, somehow.

Our leaders decided that we were going to camp for the night in the deserted village.

One of the B-24s in Bill's outfit

Slight battle damage

CHAPTER 17

Rolling Rivers and Steep Hills

Sleep escaped me that night. The images of the dead weighed on my mind, and exhaustion weighed on my body. Around me, everyone had fallen asleep, using the hard ground for beds and stones for pillows. One of the rebels kept watch on the roof of one of the houses.

My eyelids could not stay open any longer, but my mind refused to rest, taking me instead to places on its own, leaving my body behind, lying on the hard, cold surface. An enormous wave lifted me up and tossed me onto another wave. Down the wide river I was carried by the waves. The river water was brown and angry. It was running in the middle of a deserted land, surrounded by brown hills and trees black in the aftermath of a great fire. Up and down the waves carried me. Then an odd calmness overtook me, as if I were used to this kind of roller coaster ride, as if I were not worried about my destination.

Suddenly, I was lying by the riverside. The sun was hot, drying my wet clothes, warming my skin. I stood up, my face unshaven, my lips chapped from thirst, my clothes ripped to pieces.

Ahead of me towered a tall mountain. It was bare

Rolling Rivers and Steep Hills

except for the very top where it had blossomed with greenery. Pretty birds flew around the trees on top of the mountain, singing cheerfully. I began to walk toward the top of the mountain. I was sure I could find water up there and fruit to eat. I was almost at the top when my legs gave out, and I began to back down. Faster and faster I walked backwards, until I was at the foot of the mountain again, back where I started. I climbed up again, determined to reach the top, only to back down again, and again, and again.

I opened my eyes. Myriads of stars surrounded the silver moon in the clear sky. I smiled about my vivid dream. It demonstrated clearly my life up to now. On this journey I had encountered rivers and climbed mountains, only to remain in uncertainty. Each daily success still left me far from contentment, just like back in my childhood, when not much made sense.

I thought about rivers and hills. I thought about the river where Frank and Mother set up their tent for us to live in for a few months. I thought about the hills in Michigan. To me, rivers offered opportunity; hills represented problems.

Thinking of rivers reminded me of the time we moved to Lowell, Michigan. Lowell was built over the Flat River, which ran under the town. All of the stores were built on pilings. The river is about two city blocks wide at this point. Old Highway M21 and the sidewalks run in front of the stores. The dam is built just downstream from the highway.

The other river, Grand River, intersects Flat River about three quarters of a mile below the town. There is a contrast between these two rivers. Beautiful, clear water coming from the north flows in Flat River. Grand River flows from the east, and is a lowland, muddy-bottom river.

Over Flat River, there were several stores. One of them, Chris's Drugs and Ice Cream Soda Fountain, was a favorite spot for all the town's kids. I will always have a warm spot in my heart for Mr. Christensen, the owner of the shop. He had a five-cent sundae for us poor kids who never had a dime. The other kids had to pay the dime.

Mother and Ray had moved to Lowell because of Bob, Ray's friend, the bean thief. Bob had gotten out of jail and moved to Lowell to work on the farms, picking peas. Of course I was dragged along with the adults. We all got jobs on a farm picking peas. Bob, Ray, and Mom were paid fifty cents a day, and I got twenty-five, but soon the peas were gone, and so were the jobs.

As for Ray, this was the only time that he held a job for over a week. Even as a nine-year-old boy, I knew that we were destitute when we began to eat home-canned cherries for breakfast, lunch, and dinner. After three days of the cherry diet, there was nothing left to eat. No one had a job, and Ray had lost his welfare money when we moved to Lowell. Since we had run out of cherries, Ray took me along to downtown Lowell, about one and a half miles from where we lived. We had no car, so it was a long walk, and being with Ray made it more unpleasant. Only when I saw the welfare agency office did I know what was up to. I was sure he had taken me along for effect. The welfare agent took pity on me and gave Ray an order for six dollars at the grocery store. Shortly after that, Ray got on regular welfare, and he stayed on it throughout his tenure as Mom's husband.

Ray was a little over six feet tall, and not much bigger than a darning needle. As a child, there were many times that I wanted to kill Ray because he was extremely and violently jealous of my mother. Many times I shut myself in my tiny room, listening to the shouting matches, with Ray spewing out all of the filth that his 56 years of hard living had taught him. He constantly accused Mom of every vile thing he could think of. I considered his behavior to be a great education for me, in what not to do in life. His voice was so loud that the neighbors, half a mile down the road complained to our landlord and we had to move again.

This time, we moved to a tiny house closer to down town. The house had no electricity. There was a coal stove for heating and cooking. I did all my studying under Mom's little Gone With the Wind kerosene lamp. At times, when we were alone, Mother held me. Her embrace warmed my heart for a while, but then Ray would start one of his tirades, and I would be filled with anger and hatred again.

Often when I came home from school, Ray would yell at me for no reason and make me sit in a straight backed chair and read the Bible for hours. I had to hold the Bible in both hands in front of me and not allow it to lie in my lap. This was a punishment and I had no idea what I had done wrong.

"Why are you letting him do this to us?" I would ask my mother when we were alone.

She would remain quiet, and often I would see a tear or two rolling from her eyes. Meanwhile, Ray continued to rant and rave, accusing Mom of having an affair with a married neighbor. I knew that there was no truth to his accusations. His jealousy and mistrust of Mother continued until we had rented practically every rental house in town. One day, Dad and Mayme came by our house, selling radishes door to door. The children, Red and Evelyn, my dearest friends, were with them. It was then that I learned that they had moved to my grandfather's farm in Middleville, Michigan, because work in Lansing and Flint was non existent. My grandfather, a crusty old German, had share farmed this sandy, stony farm for several years. Grandpa's wife had died in her 36th year, after having eleven children. I begged my mother to let me go and stay on the farm. There at least I would have Red and Evelyn to play with, and of course I would be away from Ray. My mother agreed to let me go.

Despite the hard work on the farm, such as hoeing the weeds in the beans and weeding onions on our hands and knees in the muck, I had a great time playing with my friends. My favorite time was when we went to nearby Lake Barlow to bathe and swim. After a hard day in the field it was a good chance to get away from my grand father's unhappy face. His demeanor did not get any better, since the price of beans was so poor that year that he couldn't even pay the II puller II charge. He had us all hand pull enough beans to get us through the winter, and then we plowed the remaining forty acres under. I felt sad as I saw our whole summer's work going back into the ground. Red, Evelyn, and I were now in middle school in Middleville. The school bus picked us up each day. Although our farm was only three miles from the school, we had to ride about fifteen miles each way in order to pick up and drop off other children. Our farm was the first and last stop. The long rides were worth it, though, because my brother Harold went to the same school, and I got to see him every day.

By now, I felt that I was in an environment that a child should belong in. Red and Evelyn and Harold made me feel like I had a family, and the school was fun because I surrounded myself with plenty of other children to play with. But just to make sure that I did not get comfortable feeling like a child, my mother and Ray showed up at the farm one day, saying that they had come to take me back. My heart saddened. I did not want to leave the farm. I begged my mother to let me stay, but she did not listen to my pleas. My mother was my legal guardian, so I had to go. I looked back from the window of the Model T

Ford Coupe watching Red and Evelyn waving good-bye until the far turn took me away from them. I thought of my brother, who would be looking for me at the school yard in the morning. I was sad that I didn't get to say good bye to him.

We headed back to Lowell in a car that Mother had borrowed from a friend. On the way, we had to go up a number of long hills. On one of the hills, the car engine stopped. The problem was that the Model T had the gas tank under the seat, and as a result of the engine being higher than the gas tank, the gas did not keep the carburetor full going up long hills. My mother let the car coast down the hill backwards until the gas tank and the engine were level. Then she would restart the engine and turn the car around, backing up all the way to the top of the hill. This happened several times, and each time we had to back down the hill, turn the car around, back up to the top, turn around again, and we were once more on our way. Of course, if the gas tank were filled with gas, this would not have been a problem. But Ray never had enough money to buy food, never mind a luxury item such as a full tank of gasoline. I came to dislike steep hills, mainly because of this ordeal. Hills meant trouble.

The rivers were a different story, because they offered good fishing, and as a kid, that was my favorite pas time. I would often catch game fish and sell them to various people who I had built up as customers.

I remember one day when I was twelve years old, I was fishing off a bridge in the center of town when I spot ted a huge black bass. The water was clear, and about twelve feet deep. I was fishing with a hellgrammite. I would let the hellgrammite go with the current, past the fish's nose. When he ignored it, I moved it over a little, and placed it

Rolling Rivers and Steep Hills

in front of his nose again. He did not appear to be hungry, but after the hellgrammite hit his nose half-a dozen times, he lost his temper and snapped it. I had a difficult time landing him, but finally pulled him over the bridge rail and onto the sidewalk. Several people had gathered around to watch me catch the big fish. A man came out from the crowd and asked for my name. After I told him, he took a ruler from his coat pocket to measure my bass. It was twenty-two inches long! The man then told me that he was a game warden. I got really scared. I had no permit for fishing, and I knew that I was going to jail for sure. But I felt relieved when the warden said that he was going to send my name and a story about my catch to a sports magazine.

I sold the big bass to Rolly, one of my customers. He owned a well-drilling rig and lived over the river. I got one dollar and fifty cents for it. Usually, I got twenty-five cents for my big catch. I knew selling game fish was illegal, but I did it all the time. I had absolutely no remorse for my illegal dealings, because I had the consolation of knowing that I was helping to put food on our table.

Lying by the ruins of homes, staring out into the clear sky with the endless stars, I wondered about rivers and hills – the rivers that I had been through, and the hills ahead of me to climb.

CHAPTER 18

Dance With Me

I had to stop wondering about the many mountains towering in front of me.

The rivers, the valleys, the villages, and the forests should not be an obstacle to my vision, the vision that was permanently engraved in my mind: to reach the land of deliverance. I felt that with every one of my steps this land was closer to me, and that made the marathon walk hopeful and bearable.

The endless miles that I had left behind had infused a superior confidence in me. The new sun did not bring uncertainty but hope. Here and now was the place and time that I realized how the human spirit could triumph over extraordinary circumstances.

The periodic flashbacks to my childhood helped me to remember another world, a world that allowed me to embrace this remote place with a bit of reality, a world away from the blood and the bullets.

It was early morning as we began our exploration into the woods. The foliage of the trees was dense and hung low in our path, the branches of the bushes sprang long and thick. They made our walk through the woods tiring and slow.

This was the second day that we went without food. Occasionally, we saw wild rabbits and deer running through the woods. The rebels lifted their guns, pretending to shoot, but they never did. They knew that gunshots would give away our position to the enemy. Walking in the woods without being detected was a test of strength, mental torment along with physical torture. It became unbearable at times, but still none of us wavered in our belief that we would come out of this alive.

As the dusk of the day settled around us, we began to search for a place to camp. The dense woods were beginning to thin out now. Our leaders pointed to a clearing and indicated to us that this was to be our home for the night.

It felt good to lie down. The mountains around us laid their shadows on the warm land. Slowly the sun disappeared and allowed darkness to blanket the earth.

Soon I fell asleep.

A chorus of singing voices ascended from the sweet earth. The melodies penetrated my ears and slowly seeped into my senses. I opened my eyes. A bright moon was now hanging from a sky full of stars. Strangely, the chorus of voices continued after I was awake, only now, it was coming from the hills. The sleeping bodies around me began to move and slowly awaken from their sleep.

"What's going on?" the men would ask with sleep in their voices.

We all stood up, uncertain what to do next. Behind us were the dense woods, ahead of us the tall mountains and hills full of singing people. Our dilemma was which way to go. I turned to get advice from our leaders. They were not there. Maybe the major or Maria would know. To my surprise, they were gone, too.

"Should we go and find out who is singing?" some one asked.

"I don't know. I would hate to get separated from our leaders," I answered.

"Maybe they went to scout out the area that the voices are coming from," someone else suggested.

"Let's wait."

We waited for about one hour. The singing from the hills continued. Finally, we decided to move toward the singing voices. In a few minutes we were out of the woods. An array of hills circled around us. On one of the hills, to our left, there were silhouettes dancing under the moon light.

"I wonder what this is all about?" I asked. "Maybe the war is over," John replied.

A ray of hope entered my heart. It was possible. We had been isolated from the civilized world for about a month now. It had been a month without news about the progress of the war, a month without the familiar sound of our language.

"Should we go and ask?" Arthur suggested.

"We don't even know who those people are. For all we know, they might be Chetniks," Clarence cautioned us.

We stood for a few moments, undecided about what we were going to do.

The singing voices and the rhythmic clapping of hands grew louder. It had been awhile since I had heard happy sounds and seen joyful people. I knew that everyone was curious to find out about the dancing shadows on the hill. The fact that we were lost without a leader made our decision easier to go to the hill.

"We must be careful," I warned them, as we approached the hill.

Somehow, I had a feeling that the Englishman, Maria, and our leaders, were somewhere among the people on the hill.

We reached the foot of the hill. On its slopes were hundreds of tall trees. The clapping continued along with shouts of triumphant celebration that accompanied the songs.

"What do you think, guys? Should we move up?" "Why not? We need a little entertainment."

Slowly we climbed the slopes. I could feel the vibration of the singing voices and the joy of dancing. I could now see several people ahead of us. We looked at each other and shrugged our shoulders and moved on toward the top of the hill. By the time we reached the top we were surrounded by dozens of jubilant people. No one seemed to pay any attention to our presence.

At the bottom of the other side of the hill there was a tiny valley. Around the valley towered other hills forming a natural amphitheater. There was a great festive scene. All around the hills dozens of people celebrated with songs and dancing.

The Last Mission

Suddenly, there was silence. In the middle of the tiny valley there was a small group of people. Three of them took out clarinets and began to weave a mournful melody on the still air. Manly voices began to rise toward the heavens, like the prayers of a cantor. The emotions of the people increased with the volume of the song. The notes became a chorus from hundreds of mouths and there was rhythmic clapping.

The tapestry of the tiny valley became a natural stage where the people began a circular dance around the musicians. I was mesmerized by the energy of the people. Since the people paid little attention to us, we felt relatively safe.

We walked through the animated crowd and headed downward. We found a spot toward the bottom of the hill and sat down. I figured that since I was unable to comprehend the meaning of this celebration I might as well enjoy the entertainment.

Suddenly, I spotted Maria among the dancing people. She was dancing with gusto and seemed to be full of joy.

She spotted us in the crowd and ran to us.

"Come on boys, dance with me!" "No, no, that's okay," we replied.

Dancing was the furthest thing from our minds.

"What is the occasion?" I asked.

"Victory, victory! Partisans have Chetniks on the run, no more Chetniks!" There was a triumphant expression in her voice, as if this were her victory.

As for me, I was glad for the Partisans and their help,

but the big war was still on, as far as we knew. Our safety was still far away, across the Adriatic Sea.

The situation in Yugoslavia was becoming clear: Tito's forces were in control. Military support from the Allies and the success of the Partisans brought Tito closer to political power. By now the Serbian guerilla forces under General Draza Mihailovic were defeated in Herzegovina and Montenegro and Mihailovic was forced to retreat to the Serbian mountains with the remnants of his command.

Morning was near. The tempo of the celebration had not lost its energy.

For us, it was time to go find our safe ground and hopefully from there go on to Italy, so that we could sing our own songs of freedom.

On the top of the hill, we joined a group of airmen, wanderers like us. I was looking for the major and Maria, as they were a big part of my adventure, responsible for keeping me safe. Maria was not there, but the one-eyed major walked up to our group.

"Keep moving south. Your leader knows the way," he said.

"And you, Major?" I asked.

"I'll stay for a while," he said. He did not smile, but he seemed less grim than usual.

"Thank you for saving my life," I said. I saluted him and then shook his hand.

After that, south we went.

CHAPTER 19

To The Land of Deliverance

A new rebel led our team of airmen southbound.

The echo of the songs and the hand clapping followed us for a while and it remained nested in my ears for a while longer.

I looked at the men walking alongside me; I saw a hero behind each unshaven face, I noticed a giant towering over the tired steps. Men walked with ripped clothes and shoes full of holes as their only possessions, men who never complained about the elements or the ordeal. They were humans whose spirits of survival soared with determination. Tremendous pride rose in my heart.

Along the way we picked up more airmen who were shot down and taken to villages nearby, men who were also anxious to reach the land of deliverance. At first, there were a few, then a few more, and then more came to join us. After a while there were about twenty of us, all Allied airmen who wore various uniforms.

Some of the people in the group were critically wounded. There was an Italian carrying another man on his back, piggyback. The man being carried was barely breathing. The man who carried him was determined to bring him home alive.

"Siamo quasi là," ("We are almost there,") he kept repeating as he struggled to keep his balance with every step.

There were four Maggie's Drawers crewmembers walking along with this group of wanderers. The fates of the other crewmembers were unknown to us. We hoped they were with similar groups, headed in the same direction. It had been two days since the panegyric, an eerie victory dance that we were glad to see, but that marked no real ending for us. We continued to hike over several mountains and pass through numerous small valleys. I was curious why I did not see any Germans in these valleys.

"They're moving all of their forces to the bigger cities," one of the airmen told me.

After a steep and difficult climb we reached the top of a hill. Looking down the southern slope we could see a large town, severely damaged from bombing and battles. The going was easier as we descended into the valley.

Walking through the ruins of the streets, I saw only a few buildings that still had roofs. The front steel shutters of the shops were either blown off or bowed.

The smell of death and the picture of absolute devastation surrounded us. Our leaders guided us through narrow streets riddled with large holes and littered with piles of rubble. The Italian airman, dragging his feet, was still carrying his friend on his back. Though he staggered under the heavy load, he displayed tremendous strength and courage.

"Siamo quit! Siamo quit!" ("We're here! We're here!")

he kept saying to his comrade.

While we moved through the destroyed town, a strange sensation came over me. At that moment I felt that I belonged to neither world.

Behind me, I left the devastation of human tragedy. Ahead of me, I had the anticipation of human rejoicing.

As the dusk of the ending day blanketed the ruined city, a colorful giddiness enveloped my mind. Behind me in the mist, I observed the world half ruined, half composed of dreams. Ahead of me was the direction toward the strong voice of hope that kept urging me to move on. Behind me there were dark, unyielding mysteries pounding in my heart, a heart that remained thirsty to discover the celebration of life.

With every step, with every inch of ground I covered, the human mystery seemed to fade into the back ground as I approached the land of deliverance.

At the far edge of the deserted town, an American colonel appeared from one of the buildings that still had a roof. He warmly welcomed us. We were taken into a building and given something to eat. The colonel informed us that this town was the end of our journey, and that from a secret airfield, we were going to be airlifted back to Italy.

We could hardly grasp the meaning of his words. We were finally under Allied control, after more than a month of danger and hardship, and we were overjoyed, except that fatigue overcame all other impulses in our minds. We stared at the officer, unsure what to do next.

"Find a place to rest," the colonel said.

It was then when I saw the familiar face of our navigator, William Birchfield. With a big smile across his face, he walked over to our group and said, "I'm so glad to see you all again!" As we shook hands, another group of air men rushed up to welcome us. I let out a big sigh of relief when I saw that Clark Fetterman, Joe Maloney and Edward O'Conner were among them. Thank God that the rest of "Maggie's" crew had made it here alive.

Our sleeping quarters were a two-story building that seemed to be an old hotel because it was divided into several small rooms. Of course, there was no furniture any where in the building. Several airmen occupied the rooms. I found a spot upstairs and lay on the floor to rest.

CHAPTER 20

A Nation of Wanderers

There were sleeping men all around me, yet I could only toss around, trying to keep my eyes closed. It was a little past midnight, and the excitement of freedom was mounting inside of me. I gave up trying to rest, and got up. I walked outside. Small groups of airmen sat around.

Some were enjoying a cigarette; others just sat quietly. I felt a strange bonding with these airmen; the feeling of camaraderie was strong. We would sacrifice our lives for one another, even though the words exchanged between us were limited. It was as if we were afraid to know one another too closely. We had lived close to the possibility of death for too long. So we had learned to maintain a safe distance, as if the pain of loss of a stranger would be less severe than that of the loss of a close friend. But the bond among us was strong and undeniable.

We were a family of wanderers in a strange land.

Against all the odds, we had survived.

The sound of plane engines came from the horizon. My first instinct was to run for cover, but I remained standing as I observed the others unmoved by the sound of the approaching aircraft. The outline of a Curtiss C-46 transport plane appeared from behind the mountains. The pilot lowered his aircraft inside of the mountaintops and dropped a few packages. Then he lifted the nose of the plane over the mountains and flew away. What was dropped on the small field was not bombs, but food. This doubled my certitude that here and now I was relatively safe. A team of airmen hiked down the hill to pick up the packages.

When dawn broke the darkness, I was still awake. I waited for the first meal at midmorning. After that, I went to my room and lay in my spot, enjoying the contentment of a full stomach.

I reminisced about my childhood, trying to collect my thoughts, to understand what gave me the strength to endure such an adventure. Everything seemed so long ago and in places so far away from here. Yet the picture was still alive in my mind, even here sitting amid rubble and the silent pain of everyone around me.

When I closed my eyes, moving pictures ran through my mind like an old movie. There was a nice school in Lowell. I remembered the streets that I ran through with my best friend Jim to get to the King Milling Company. There we collected bags full of corncobs from the cob bin. Several of us poor kids ran to the cob bin with bags. We had to get there first to take as much as we could carry. Jim and I sold the corncobs to the businesses around town that used them as kindling to start fires, since every one in town had a coal stove or furnace. They would pay us ten cents a bag in the wintertime and five cents in the summer.

The Last Mission

Jim and I were partners in other jobs, as well. In the bowling alley we would set up the pins on four lanes. We worked until midnight. We got paid two cents a line and occasionally would pick up a quarter thrown down the alley by a wealthy bowler. That is where I got a lot of exercise because I had to hurry and pick up all the downed pins and clear the alley before the next ball came. The jump run-pick-get-out-of-the-way process continued for hours. Then, there was the clam picking from the clear waters of the Flat River. That was a skillful job. The clams or mussels buried themselves in the riverbed. The only part we could see through the glass of our peeker box was their feelers waving in the moving water. The peeker box was made out of a wood frame about one foot square with a glass bottom.

My fishing tool was a three-foot long rod with a flattened end; it looked just like a golf club. When I spotted through the glass and saw the mussels' antennae waving, I quickly inserted the flat end of the poker-rod into the opening of the mussel. Under the impact of the rod the shellfish closed, trapping the poker inside its shell. Then I pulled it up from the river bottom and deposited it in a wash tub that was tied to my waist.

When the tub was filled, I floated it back to our campsite where a "cooker" was set up.

The "cooker" was a container placed on cement blocks. When we had filled the cooker, we added water and started a fire under it. For the fire we used old cut up tires.

We covered the mussels with burlap sacks to hold the

steam in. After they were fully steamed and opened up, the mussels were shoveled out onto a makeshift sorting table.

My partner Jim and I extracted the meat and fed it to the fish. The shells were sorted out into #1 and #2 qualities and placed in burlap bags. The shell buyers for the button factory paid three cents per pound for the good ones and one cent per pound for the #2 shells. Jim and I got to watch, once, as the workers dumped loads of shells into big galvanize II horse tanks II in the basement of the factory. When the shells were soft, big machines cut button blanks by the thousands. Then they were shipped off to different factories where buttons were made from them.

I spent entire summers shelling on the river.

In our spare time from shelling, Jim and I went around picking up aluminum, brass, copper and iron items from trashcans. We sold them to John Kellogg's junkyard, where Old John paid a few cents per pound. The price varied depending on the metal.

Those years I spent the least amount of time possible at home. I was practically growing up on my own. I felt that people like Old John Kellogg, and Harvey Hatsmer, another junk dealer, cared more about me than my step father did. Old John gave me work on Saturdays. He trusted me to weigh junk, papers, and cardboard that other kids brought in.

At the age of fifteen I was working full time for Old John and Harvey. That was when I got my first car.

A man drove a 1926 Model T Ford into the yard

one day to sell for junk. I wanted to buy it and Old John let me take it for a test drive.

Three blocks away the uphill slope was too much for the old car. It began to back down the hill. From the corner of my eye, I saw the sheriff's car coming over the top of the hill. I knew I was in trouble. I let off the brakes and my car rolled backward at full speed and eventually got out of control, running off the dirt road.

I was trapped between two desperate elements, trying to bring the car under control and fleeing to escape the sheriff. Usually, when you are desperate, things turn to drama or comedy or both.

As the car went off the road and the rear axle hit a big rock, the right wheel was lifted off the ground and I was thrown out of the car and was lying on my stomach. When I finally lifted my head, I was faced with the sheriff's boots. Slowly I lifted my eyes, afraid to discover the expression on his face.

"Why don't you get up?" His voice matched his surly face.

I did get up.

"I suppose you have no driver's license."

I hung my head down in shame.

"And I see that your car has no license plates."

I thought that I was going to jail for sure as the sheriff lectured me for a while.

I stood in silence.

"Take this damned junk heap back to Old John!"

"Yes sir."

"And don't let me catch you driving again!" "No sir"

But the seduction of driving your first car is overwhelming. So, I did sneak in a few drives around the junk yard. That was after I bought the car from Old John. The price was a whopping six dollars. I gave Old John one dollar down and I was to pay him one dollar a month. I fixed the car and it ran fairly well.

During one of my drives around the yard there was a knocking in the engine.

"A rod has gone out," Old John said and gave me back my dollar.

Old John gave me one dollar to junk the car and with great disappointment I turned my first car into junk. When I was sixteen years old I hitchhiked to Grand Rapids and, with the two dollars I had saved, got my driver's license. I was now a man, and a man needs a car. My friend, Jim, told me that his uncle had traded in his 1926 Chevrolet two door and that it was available at the local Chevrolet dealer for twelve dollars.

The first time that I fell in love was at the car dealer's lot when I saw that 1926 Chevrolet. It was a dark green vision, the most beautiful thing in the whole world. The dealer wanted six dollars down and the rest in twenty days.

I had four dollars and borrowed two from Old John.

As I drove the car out of the lot I felt like I was flying between soft white clouds.

Twenty days later I became frantic. I was short three

dollars for my final payment. The thought that I could lose my car kept me awake the night before. I remembered an older rich boy who was looking for new tires. My Chevrolet had brand new tires on it.

The next morning I sold him my two new front tires for three dollars. He was even happy to let me have his two old front tires.

I put the old tires on my car and rushed to the car dealer and made my last payment. Now I had a clear title to my precious jewel. An overwhelming sense of triumph came over me.

Now, in the early morning darkness, I felt some thing similar to that triumphant feeling, only much stronger.

Growing up in Lowell, Michigan, had been hard for me, but not much different than for lots of other poor kids around the country. We scrounged for nickels, we worked long and hard for not much, and we took pleasure in our small victories. I smiled at the picture in my mind of the kid selling shells and corncobs. I could almost feel the wind blowing in my hair as I drove that Chevy around. Life had not always been kind, but I had learned to work. I had learned to keep on working, even when I was tired or when I would rather be playing. And, I had learned to be resourceful. Above all, it seemed, my life had been about changes. I was always moving around, always going to new schools and meeting new people, always finding ways to earn a living. Not a bad education, I thought to myself, for a guy who ended up having to count on pure endurance to survive. I had always struggled to find ways to pull some kind of meaning from the losses and hardships I had been dealt. This trip from being shot down to finally coming back to safety, had been no different.

I opened my eyes and looked around me.

Men were resting in the rubble and ruin, destruction that man himself had inflicted on the world.

But I knew full well that every one of us who had struggled to survive this adventure echoed my sentiment to build a kinder, more peaceful world.

CHAPTER 21

In Anticipation of Freedom

This was an inactive day. I lazily sat around the building talking with the other airmen, sharing stories, anticipating the moment of freedom. It felt odd that I did not have to get up and begin walking again. The marathon was finally over.

That night, thinking of freedom, I fell into a deep, sweet sleep. I awoke very early the next morning. All around me, people were wandering, waiting for destiny to take its course.

Our most bonding duty was to take off our shirts and flight suit tops, and sit in a circle and count the lice that we picked off of our clothes. Once we were certain that all of the lice were picked off, we put our clothes back on. A few minutes later I could feel a louse skate around my ribcage.

The day went on uneventfully. We all waited impatiently in anticipation of being called for lift-off standby. I felt fortunate that I was one of the few to reach this secret lift-off location. This was the gateway to the promised land, where all rescued airmen were taken to be airlifted back to various locations in Italy. Thousands of airmen did not

In Anticipation of Freedom

make it to this airfield. Their lives ended in the steep mountains, the dangerous valleys, or in prison camps.

Then, I thought of the many other people whose lives had been affected by this war.

In the destroyed city where we stayed there were no natives. The rebels who had brought us here had gone back to gather more fallen airmen. The original inhabitants of the city were either dead or had been taken away to German forced labor camps.

An announcement by a young airman forced me to leave these thoughts behind. He was reading the list of people on today's lift-off roster. I heard my name called. Today, it was my turn to be excited. My gaze focused on the little valley below the ruined city where we waited.

The hidden airfield was a grassy valley, completely surrounded by high mountains. I wondered how a C-46 could possibly land in that valley, coming over the steep mountaintops. The pilot would have to have extraordinary skills to be able to successfully land an aircraft in that field.

It was eleven o'clock that night when, along with thirty-two others, I walked the two miles down to the valley airfield. It was a night covered with fog, and the sky was loaded with heavy clouds.

Our trek over the rough terrain was tiring. We reached the airfield and were ordered to wait on the east side of the field.

The dark clouds hung so low that they covered the mountaintops. The fog was thick and did not allow me to see beyond the middle of the airfield. There was no possible way that an aircraft would be able to land under these conditions. But I did not give up hope.

We stood intently, listening for the sound of an airplane.

The sound came shortly afterward. It was the familiar drone of the C-46 or C-47 engines.

The plane could be heard above the dark clouds and when it was directly overhead our commander shot up a red flare. The red flare indicated to the pilot that visibility was bad and the landing had to be cancelled. The fleeting disappointment was replaced with renewed hope that the next midnight a landing would be successful.

We hiked back to our billets.

I shared a room with six others. By now we had built temporary beds by nailing old boards to 2 by 4 sup ports against the wall. It took me awhile to find sleep that night. In my mind, I created a lift-off with me aboard. I imagined the flight between the clouds, and that now I would be flying over the Adriatic Sea. I fell asleep with the feeling of freedom intact in my heart.

Images of barefooted people walking on soft grass visited my sleep that night. Natives of Yugoslavia appeared on the highest mountain summits. They were dancing the circular dance of freedom. The sky was clear and deep blue. The natives signaled to me to join their dance.

As I began my steps toward them, the sky darkened. A flock of giant black birds flew overhead, so close I could

In Anticipation of Freedom

touch them. Thunder and lightning shook the sky. Voices from behind me urged me to run. The voices sounded surreal.

"Let's go! Let's go! Move out!" This time, the voices were real.

I jumped off my board bed and began to run to the stairs. By the time I hit the bottom of the stairs I was wide awake and alert to what was happening. Bombs were falling. The concussion from one blew me backward onto the stairs. Tiles from the roof rained down on me.

I stood up and ran barefoot over the broken tile. In a few seconds I was outside and found myself among several running men. I went over a five-foot fence without touching the wire. I was in mid-air when the third bomb exploded. I fell into a slit trench with shrapnel and dirt flying around me. More bodies fell into the trench.

I looked up to the sky. A Ju-88 was taking his time dropping bombs on us. He made a slow turn, came back over the same path, and dropped three more five hundred pound bombs. One of the bombs fell on our building. People were still running for safety. I checked with the people around me in the trench as the enemy plane picked up speed and disappeared far into the horizon. None of them were injured.

Some of the others who were not able to make it to the trench suffered shrapnel wounds.

Thank God everyone was alive.

We went back to our building to check the damage.

Everything was covered in debris and stones. Our bed room now matched all the rest of the town's buildings: it had no roof.

When night fell we marched back to the airfield. The sky was once again completely covered by clouds.

A ray of hope made my heart beat in anticipation of flying away from here. I heard the engines and then I saw the red flare shooting up to the sky.

The ray of hope would have to wait for tomorrow.

"How many tomorrows?" I wondered, as I returned to our billet and lay in my open-roofed room. There I found myself praying for a clear night.

In Anticipation of Freedom

LOWELL, MICHIGAN, MAX 25, 1944

Lost Over Europe, "Found" in Lowell

Lowell—Reported missing last month over Europe, S/Sgt. William Kollar, 24, Friday morning knocked at the door of his mother's home and announced he had a 21-day furlough. His mother, Mrs. Dave Woudwyck, had received no word about him since the war department included his name on the missing list.

Kollar, a graduate of Lowell High school, was a gunner on an army bomber serving with the 15th air forces in Italy. He reported that his plane was shot down while on a mission. One crew member was killed; one was captured and eight others, aided by the underground, walked for weeks before reaching safety.

The sergeant has been wounded twice and has received the air medal and the purple heart. He has been in the army since April, 1942.

CHAPTER 22

Lift-off

As I lay on the floor I watched the sky. Dark clouds remained stubbornly between the heavens and me. I fell asleep, hoping that tomorrow, I would be able to clearly see the moon and stars.

The next night, despite my prayers, clouds covered the sky again.

We made our trek to the airfield anyway. Thirty three airmen stood quietly at the end of the airfield, expecting the same routine: the engine drone, the red flare, and the long walk back.

I heard the sound of the plane's engines and I sensed the excited heartbeats around me. Looking up to the sky I observed the clouds standing graceless and stubborn. The roar of the engines grew louder.

My eyes were glued to the sky. Suddenly, I noticed a small opening. The clouds seemed to part like curtains, as if God had waved His hand and opened a window for us. By the time the aircraft was above us, the break in the clouds was about one hundred yards wide.

I held my breath, thinking that the moment of redemption had arrived.

Lift-off

"A miracle," someone whispered.

I watched our commander lifting up his gun to shoot the flare. The lifting of his hand toward the sky seemed to me to be in slow motion. My eyes followed the barrel of the gun. Finally, the flare came out.

It was green, green and bright. Green was the color of freedom.

In a few seconds, the C-46 came through the opening in the clouds at a very steep angle. The pilot leveled off the plane inside the mountain range, made a circle, and pointed the nose down for a landing.

He taxied to our end of the field with the door open. The crew chief on the plane was throwing out supplies while the plane was moving, and the team of airmen who had escorted us down to the field was retrieving the boxes and crates.

"Let's go, go, go! Move, move, move!" the colonel urged us.

We needed no urging. All of us were off and running. It took about three minutes for all of us to jump onboard. Then the pilot gave it full power and headed directly at a cliff.

With every second that passed, the cliff was coming closer. I held my breath and we all held onto one another preparing for the crash. We were just a few yards away from the cliff when the pilot pulled the nose up sharply. The overloaded plane creaked as it labored upward. Just as I was thinking of the possibility of the plane breaking down, there was a loud crash on the left side of the plane.

A rush of cold air filled the plane.

"Hold on," voices cautioned. We did just that, holding on to anything we could find.

Under the extreme strain on the fuselage, the cargo door had opened. The pressure of the wind broke it off and blew it away.

Over the commotion of unbalanced bodies, I saw the plane barely clearing the cliff. The pilot circled inside the mountain range and then the plane was wrapped in the clouds.

We were not out of danger yet.

The pilot pulled the nose of the aircraft up, undertaking the difficult and uncertain task of clearing the mountaintops. I knew that every second the plane held its nose up there was a possibility of a crash. We all sat helplessly, directing our faith and prayers at the pilot.

Suddenly, the plane leveled off and headed west. At first, I let out a sigh of relief, and then I was overcome with admiration for the pilot. Without question, this was the most skillful piloting I had ever witnessed.

Soon, we left the heavy clouds behind us, but our situation was still dangerous. The pilot had to fly at a low altitude in order to avoid detection by German radar. This was a cargo plane; it was not equipped for combat.

When we finally sighted the Adriatic Sea, we broke

Lift-off

out into wild cheers. We were well on our way to freedom. We turned to thank the crew of the cargo plane. It was only then that I noticed familiar faces.

This was the same crew that had flown the crew of Maggie's Drawers from Casablanca to Manduria, Italy, when we were on our way to report for duty. I remembered them well because shooting craps on the bucket seat of the plane had bonded us.

It was the same pilot who had impressed me back then, when we made a stop to pick up a load of ammunition. To land, he had to touch ground, fly over the dip, touch ground again, fly over another dip, and then finally set it down. After loading the ammunition, he turned the aircraft back to the dirt runway and, through landings and flying over dips, lifted the plane back up into the sky. That experience was the most exciting landing and takeoff that I had witnessed in my young flying career.

Now he was flying a group of survived airmen back to Italy, among them eight of Maggie's drawers crewmembers.

CHAPTER 23

Ghosts of the Past

*T*he drunkenness of freedom ran high in my veins during the flight from Yugoslavia to Italy. I was so anxious to step onto friendly soil that every moment of the flight seemed endless.

When the plane's tires touched the ground, and I felt the bumps of the landing, I seemed to be reborn. Everyone around me was ecstatic. We all shouted, rejoicing and embracing in celebration.

As the plane reduced speed and rolled off the runway onto the tarmac apron near the control tower, airmen waved at us, welcoming us home. Those airmen had clean uniforms and good shoes. I don't know what made me think of that. Maybe it was because I still wore my flight suit, soiled and ripped, with the cut-off legs. I looked at my military boots and thought of Goran. God bless him.

I had not shaved or bathed for days, and I felt as if I were coming back from time travel, returning from a land that existed long ago.

As I stepped down from the plane and experienced the sounds and the energy of the airport and the vehicles driving around, I felt for a moment that I was observing a strange and distant world. It was in Bari, Italy, that the plane that lifted us to freedom had landed. It almost felt surreal to hear people speaking a familiar language. There were jeeps and trucks everywhere. The noise and bustle of the airport had replaced the quietness and peace of the mountains.

Among the vehicles there were several ambulances to take us directly to the hospital. There we were housed in a secure section. First, we had to get rid of the lice through a de-lousing steam bath. My first shower for over a month was one of the most enjoyable aspects of this rediscovered civilization.

At the shower exit, we were given hospital gowns and then taken to the emergency room for treatment. Those who were severely injured were hospitalized. The rest of us were led to the mess hall for coffee, milk and doughnuts. There were more pleasant surprises besides the seductive aroma of the coffee and the smell of the dough nuts. There were tables and chairs, glasses and plates. And while anticipating the mouthwatering treat, the fact suddenly hit me that I was free! What a glorious feeling that was. The feeling of freedom now had taken a new dimension in my heart.

The experience of the past month affirmed my conviction that freedom was the kernel of my being. The monumental events of the recent past now suddenly seemed like a bad dream, a dream that I knew was true and one that I would never forget.

After coffee and doughnuts, with happy stomachs we were shown to guarded tents. These tents were set up in a secluded area of the hospital grounds. I lay down slowly on my army cot. I had not slept in a bed for thirty-four nights. When the clean sheets wrapped around my clean body, I felt a sweet embrace that brought a smile to my face.

I closed my eyes. I envisioned the land that I had left behind, miles and miles of it – how many exactly I did not know – but for certain there were hundreds of miles that my steps had covered. There were endless mountaintops I had to climb, peaks that at the moment were obstacles to my freedom. However, now I could look back and remember the beauty, the green trees, the rills of clear water, the wild birds, and the rugged countryside.

I remembered the valleys that I had to cross, devastated for sure by man's incompetence to communicate and get along with his fellow man. Now I could see the green grass, the daisies, and the poppies that I had left behind. I remembered the deep blue skies of the nights that were embroidered with a myriad of stars. I could feel the crisp air on the mountaintops. I remembered the natural beauty of the country.

I could not forget the kind faces of the wonderful folks who generously shared with me the little that they had. It was that little bit that kept me alive and gave me strength to walk farther. I made a conscious decision to embrace the beauty of life and let the pain remain a ghost of the past.

In our secluded, area we were given strict orders not to discuss our activities of the past month with anyone and were told that we would be in isolation for individual debriefing. My debriefing was the next day. Three officers met me in one of the tents.

At first, they congratulated me and expressed great admiration for the fact that I had survived the wilderness and the enemy. They wanted to know all the details of our mission, of how we got shot down and what I had seen. They took some notes on my account of the long march, and of the rebels who had protected and guided us. Then, they stressed the great importance of disclosing nothing to anyone about our rescue, or about the details of the ordeal I experienced in enemy territory.

"The safety of hundreds of airmen depends on the secrecy of that airfield and the method of retrieval," one of the officers said.

"Revealing any details about your rescue will result in court martial," another added.

"It is only when you are notified in writing, that you will be able to discuss your experiences. Until such a letter arrives in your hands, you are under a gag order," the third one added.

After debriefing, we were given new uniforms. Mine was considerably smaller than the one I wore before my last mission, because I had lost so much weight. When I had my set of khakis on, tears clouded my eyes as I realized what a great honor it was to serve my country, and to be an American. That moment was one of the proudest of my life.

After a few days in Bari, our crew was loaded onto another plane and, along with several other airmen, was sent back to our base in Lecce, Italy.

Our arrival at the base turned out to be a great homecoming. Everyone looked at us as if they were seeing ghosts.

It turned out that a war correspondent who was flying on the plane next to us during the bombing mission had reported that our plane had lost a wing and crashed into the mountainside with all of us inside.

Following is the report of Newbold Noyes, Jr., of The Washington Star. "Mary" is the code name for Maggie's Drawers.

THE SUNDAY STAR, Washington, D. C.
SUNDAY, APRIL 1944

Star Correspondent Describes Aerial 'Battle of the Alps'

Noyes Flies in Second Wave of Fleet That Bombed Steyr, Downed 157 Planes

From the flight deck of a Liberator bomber Newbold Noyes, jr., a member of The Star staff, last Sunday saw the destruction of the big German ball-bearing works at Steyr, Austria. The planes had to fight for their lives over the Alps en route back to their bases. This was no ordinary mission, and the Luftwaffe came up to fight in dead earnest. When the day's total was counted, 157 enemy planes had been destroyed and the Americans had lost 36. Mr. Noyes' story is a thrilling chapter of the part America is playing in the air war over Europe.

By NEWBOLD NOYES, Jr.
Star War Correspondent.

EIGHTH ARMY 3d BOMBER BASE, Italy, April 3 (Delayed).—"Terrific" is the word for yesterday's raid on the Austrian factory town of Steyr. It met more fighter opposition than any previous raid by the 15th United States Air Force. It featured an epic running battle in which the cream of the Luftwaffe fighters pitted themselves against the ponderous power of our bomber formations, fought like demons—and lost. We used more planes that day and dropped more bombs than ever before. From a bombing point of view, the victory was decisive and devastating.

It was the kind of thing that has to be seen to be believed. I saw it.

This is the story of how the Steyr raid—and the subsequent "battle of the Alps"—looked from the flight deck of one Liberator in the second wave of the attack.

Target Already Smoking.

From 20 miles away we could see the target already half covered by smoke. The first wave of the attack obviously was doing its work well, but the target was still fighting desperately to defend itself. Steyr crouched beneath a canopy of flak hitting at the planes which were dropping their bombs on it—waiting for us.

The commander of the group I was with said something in our dawn briefing which I kept remembering in those long minutes while we closed in on the object of our mission. He had said:

"We'll have hundreds of heavy bombers and fighters in that general area, which means there will be a helluva lot of guns in the air. We are going up there and dare those guys to come out and fight. That's

(See NOYES, Page A-5.)

Noyes

(Continued From First Page.)

what we want because, we've got plenty of guns and a lot of eager beaver boys just itching for a scrap."

It was a good fight talk. I kept remembering it then, though, because the Thunderbolts and Lightnings escorting us to the target had met enemy fighters on the way and at that moment were battling it out—miles away. So now the gauntlet was being thrown down so far as we were concerned by the great formations of bombers alone and there was not a man in our ship—or in any of our ships—who did not know that the Luftwaffe was bound to take the dare.

Ship Among Veterans.

Our plane, Little Joe Jr., piloted by Lt. Mike Meger of Crivitz, Wis., led the third box of our group. We were in good company. On our right wing and slightly behind us, steady as a rock in the No. 2 position, was Big Operator, well-scarred veteran of many battles like the one which lay ahead: Big Operator, which had flown 33 consecutive missions without once having to turn back before the job was done. The No. 3 ship in the same position on our left was another good teammate in a fight. We could see the face of the man behind the waist gun grim in his helmet and oxygen mask. The whole airplane seemed to bristle, challenging the sky around us. Painted on its nose was a recumbent girl and the name—we'll call it Mary.

Three ships in a similar V formation behind it completed our box. Six such boxes flying in two attack units made the group. Off to the right and lower down another large formation was moving in on the target. It was to be a little ahead of us. Out in front was still another group approaching the target.

We banked left at about 20,000 feet and squared away for the smoking town. The Alps stretching out to the south shimmered snow white in the sunlight. Our earphones crackled and the gunner's voice came over the roar of the motors: "Here come two fighters taking off on an airfield in the valley below."

Sees Ship Break in Two.

We were watching the formation ahead, which was now in the flak. Suddenly one bomber sheered off from the formation. Something was on fire in one of its wings—a motor or a fuel tank. It went into a spin. It was a long way off, but we could see it quite clearly. It made five or six turns, then it broke in two just back of the center of the fuselage. The pieces fell. We watched for parachutes but could not see any.

A few seconds later the antiaircraft fire came up at us. Black bursts, yellow at the core, filled the sky ahead and red balls of fire floated earthward. The formation roared on through the smoke.

The earphones crackled: "Fighters, fighters coming in."

Streaking out of nowhere, the tiny planes attacked the group in front of us. There probably were not more than five or six of them but they looked like a swarm of hornets as they darted through their own flak around the tight packed formation. It held its course and 360 guns fought back, bullet for bullet with interest.

All at once where there had been a fighter there was a brilliant red flash from which the ship emerged spinning and burning. It dropped fast out of our line of vision.

We were on the bombing run then. Our bomb bay doors were open. The air around us was full of flak bursts but Mike, sitting as quietly as a man in a barber's chair, held Little Joe absolutely steady and the formation bored its way through.

"Bombs away" and we broke away fast. We banked sharp left while the bomb bay doors were still closing and in a few seconds we found ourselves out of the flak.

Describes Rocket Planes.

Then Mike's voice very sharp came over the earphones.

"Pilot to nose gunner; for God's sake what about those planes coming in at 10 o'clock. Let them have it."

Two Junkers 88s were approaching from the left and slightly below us. It was hard to judge distances in the air but I should say they were about 500 yards away when Mike spoke. A second later Little Joe shuddered slightly and the muffled clatter of our forward guns could be heard. At that instant there came streaks of flame from under the wings of the two approaching planes.

It takes a little time to say, but what I am telling you was over quite literally before you could say "rocket gun." From these streaks of flame fiery missiles about the size of spitballs hurtled toward our formation. All of them at first appeared to be heading directly at us. We were not hit, though. During the entire battle our ship was not scratched.

Mary was not so lucky. Two of its engines were knocked out. Staggering, the battered ship held its position in the formation for a few minutes and then suddenly it was gone.

A thing like that strikes close to home. I remember that when we were on the way up Mike was worried because at one time nobody seemed to be beside us on the left. When Mary showed up there after a few minutes, he had smiled and waved across at the boy who was flying her.

Hundreds of Foe Appear.

And so it went for more than half an hour. A long time to be out in the cold blue, four miles above the Alps. Tired, proud Americans spitting defiant steel at all comers, slugging it out on the long voyage home. The Luftwaffe's best—hundreds of them—the fast, deadly Messerschmitts and Focke-Wulfs and Junkers 88's slashing in and out between the groups, sometimes closing to within 25 yards, swarming all over the formation, determined to stop it.

In the course of the battle something hit the lead plane of one of the elements of the formation on our right. The Liberator blew up—flying into pieces before our eyes. Part of it—probably a motor—struck the ship on its right, shearing off the nose just forward of the wing. The second plane went into a spin. One wing and a part of its tail came off. The wreckage of the two planes fell on a third, which swerved sharply to the left out of its formation and a moment later started to spin. We could see this third ship all the way down. It did not disintegrate or burn—it simply spun to the earth. When it struck the ground, perhaps a minute after being hit, it was immediately enveloped in a black cloud of smoke. It was too far away to see whether any parachutes emerged at the last minute.

The Last Mission

Almost everyone on the base gathered around us for information about our quest for survival. There was not much we could tell them except that we had to bail out and guerrillas helped us to evade capture by the Germans.

I felt a bit uneasy about the fact that I could not reveal the details of an adventure that I had proudly survived. But my orders were strict: the details of my ordeal would be revealed only after the release of the gag order from my superior.

Ghosts of the Past

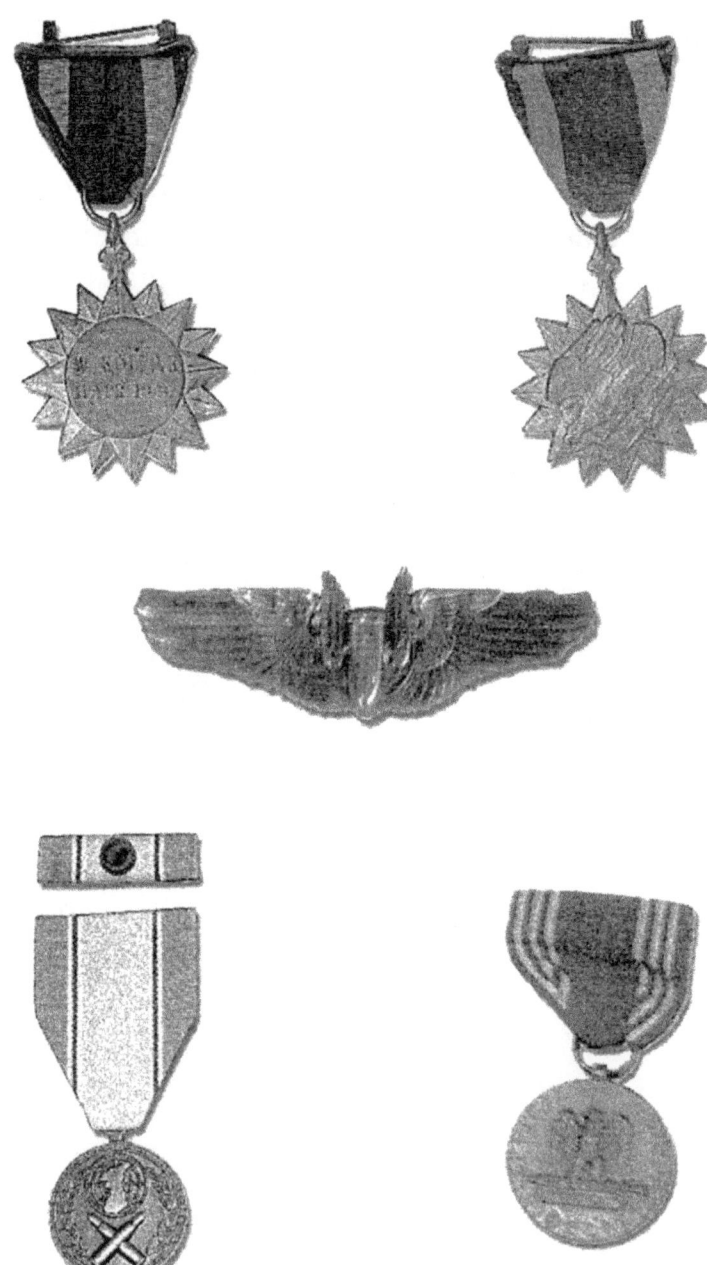

CHAPTER 24

Proud Moments

I was surprised to discover that all of my belongings were missing. My first thought was that they had been picked up by supply for safekeeping. On the first afternoon in Lecce, our crew chief showed up in my tent.

"What did they do with my stuff? ff I asked him.
"First things first, Bill," he said. "Do you remember trusting me with something before your last mission?"

I could not remember. My last mission seemed so long ago.

"No, not really, I can't remember," I replied.

The crew chief read my perplexed expression. He smiled and pulled a folded twenty-dollar bill out of his wallet.

"You trusted me with this before you left, and somehow I knew that you would be back," he told me.

I remembered now. The "loan" of a twenty-dollar bill had been a ritual of mine, before I left for a mission. It was an assurance that I was coming back, and once again it had worked.

"Now about your belongings," he said, ff they were stolen." His comments caught me off guard. Then he told me the story of Waldo.

Waldo was a young man who was one of our original crewmembers. He held the ball turret gunner position.

Proud Moments

Waldo was grounded because of medical reasons. It was because of that reason that he had been left behind on our last mission, and in order to make him useful, they had trusted him to guard our tents and belongings.

When we did not return from our mission and the news spread that we were killed, he stole everything that belonged to our crew and sold it. Waldo was later discharged from the service.

I shook the ground crew chief's hand with pride and thanked him for his faith that he would see me alive. The loss of a few personal belongings seemed not to matter, much, compared to my survival, and to the loyalty of a trusted friend.

The second day after our arrival at the base, the commander called our crew in. He had ordered a small parade in our honor.

As the airmen marched past us, I felt a great sense of pride. When they gave "eyes right" in salute, I stood erect across from the American flag that waved steadily in the breeze. I raised my arm to return the salute.

A small band played the National Anthem. The base commander stood in front of each of us, pinned the medals on our uniforms, and then saluted and congratulated us.

When the Purple Heart medal was pinned on my uniform, it seemed like a dream, a dream that I did not want to wake up from. The Purple Heart is awarded to combat-wounded personnel of all armed services. I had never envisioned such a moment, and I had hoped never to have this honor bestowed upon me. The Purple Heart was added to my air medal with its two oak leaf clusters, one for each enemy aircraft that I had shot down.

The next day, we boarded a flight back to the United States. None of our crewmembers would be allowed back into the European Theater of War. German Intelligence had our names and if we happened to be shot down again, anywhere in Europe, and caught by the Germans, we would be considered spies and executed.

During my trip back to the States, I thought about my mother. I was not surprised to find that I was missing her.

While I was growing up, I was not too close to my parents. My mind traveled back to the times before my military years, when I was trying to make some sense of my life and to understand the people whom I addressed as family members. There was not much ground for respect. My parents were two people who were caught up in their own struggles in life. For me, they were two people who gave me birth, hard times and worries. That was all. My adventures in Yugoslavia taught me many lessons. One of them was to see things from a different perspective. Some times we are in an environment where all of our energy is projected toward the task of survival and we neglect our responsibilities of compassion and love.

Laying back on the seat of the plane that was taking me home, I smiled as I reminisced about my adolescent years.

Dating was always a problem for me because I never had money to take girls out on real dates. Most of the girls did not want to spend their dates fishing off the downtown bridge. Besides, at that time, I was more concerned about working to help my mother and nursing my passion for cars.

My work was always around cars. For a while, I worked for a car dealer, Cecil Jones. He sold used cars out of the basement garage under the town's funeral home. I was making a dollar a day. My job was to clean parts and run errands.

My cars were many. Some cars I lost because I would find myself jobless due to the high unemployment of the decade of the 1930's, like my beautiful '32 two door Chevy that was repossessed after Cecil Jones let me go because business became really slow.

I had close contact with my brother, Harold, who had remained with my Uncle John on the farm in Middleville. Harold now had a Model A Ford Roadster and a Model T Ford Speedster parked on the farm. Harold let me use the old Speedster. That car was so old that it had boards on the frame for a seat. Though it had no body or fenders, for me what mattered was that I had wheels again. I built a small box behind the gas tank for junking purposes.

With money that I made from junking, I added a Stromburg 8-cylinder Dodge downdraft carburetor and a Bosch ignition system to the old Ford. Then I soldered a tire valve stem into the gas cap. Each morning, with a hand pump, I pumped a little air pressure into the tank in order to push the gas up to my big carburetor, which sat much

The Last Mission

higher than the gas tank.

And, of course, all along the way I had my run-ins with the sheriff. He often chewed me out and threatened to take away my license if I did not stop racing on Main Street, and slamming on my brakes in front of City Hall in order to make a sliding u-turn.

In the meantime, the situation at home had gotten worse.

My stepfather continued to scream obscenities at my mother, and if I ever tried to def end her he became extremely angry with me. As I grew older, I became less fearful of him. I felt that now was the time for me to stand up and protect my mother.

One day, I surprised him. During one of his temper tantrums, I grabbed him and said. "That's enough! Don't you ever raise your voice at my mother again," I pointed my fist right in his face.

After I let him go, he got a piece of chalk and marked off half of the house as his. Mother and I had the other half. From that day on, things changed around the house. Ray became less abusive and my mother became more confident. She filed for a divorce and Ray went on his way.

About a year later, my mom met Dave Woudwyk and married him. Dave treated my mother with love and respect. He and I got along great.

My favorite game at that time was Screeno. It was played at the local movie theater every Tuesday night after the movie. One particular Tuesday night, I hit the jackpot.

Proud Moments

The payoff was $75. I was a rich man.

After this experience I was introduced to real gambling. I went to work for "Pop," who owned the local pool hall. In the back of the hall, serious poker games thrived at night. Gambling was illegal but no one ever bothered us.

My job was to rake a quarter from every pot for the house, and change the deck of cards for a new one every so often.

During the day, Pop had me practice on the pool table until I was good enough to play for the house against any player who came willing to bet for a game of pool. Eventually, Pop sold the pool hall and I was out of work.

When I was sixteen, I joined the Civilian Conservation Corps and was sent to Platteville, Wisconsin, where log and brush dams were being built. Most of my money was sent to my mother. I got to keep five dollars a month for spending money.

During the wintertime, the cold in Wisconsin became unbearable, so I left the bitter winter behind and started back home to Lowell.

Soon after that, I went to work for the Works Progress Administration, another government project. I was fortunate enough to get a job in Lowell where a new bridge was to be built across the river in front of the stores, as well as a complete new dam in the same location. My pay was $32.50 a week.

I was looking forward to working hard, because this job would mean work for several years. It was there that I had the accident that severely burned my leg. It was there that my life changed when I heard the news about the Pearl Harbor tragedy.

My thoughts were interrupted as the plane landed on American soil, in New Jersey.

I was given fifteen days' furlough. I picked up the payphone to call my mother. She almost fainted at the sound of my voice. She thought that I was dead because the Red Cross had not yet notified her that I was back in Allied control.

At my arrival home, she ran to me and held me tightly. She was in tears, and elated to see me. At that moment, I felt the true love my mother had for me, and this brought me closer to her.

I was truly glad that finally had happened.

Proud Moments

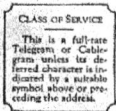

No 8 GD NB   43 Govt   WUX Washington DC   2.4% PM 3/24/44

Mrs Pearl Woudwyke
   206 Divn St
Lowell Mich

The Secretary of War desires me to express his deep regret that your son Stall Sargent William M Kollar has been reported missing in action since Two April over Austria If further details or other information are received you will be promptly notifies

         Dunlop Acting The Ajt General

CHAPTER 25

A New Life

My mother had many questions about my thirty four day disappearance. The urge to tell her everything was strong but, I had to learn not to reveal the details of the Yugoslavian undertaking to anyone. My orders about that were strict. I had to restrain myself and bury within me the details of my survival in the most private bank of my mind.

I spent my time off resting and visiting with my family.

The time came to report to my new assignment as an aerial gunner instructor at Harlingen, Texas. My new task was to fly in a B-24 bomber with students who were ready to practice firing 50-caliber guns with live ammunition.

On one of those missions with six of my students, as we were headed back to the base I noticed oil pouring out of engine #4.

"We are losing oil from engine #4!" I warned the pilot through the intercom.

Of course, the pilot could see that the temperature was going up and that the oil pressure was dropping.

"I know, I know, we can fly on three engines," he replied.

But, my concern was that the engine would soon overheat and catch fire.

"You must get #4 engine feathered before we lose all the oil," I warned him.

The pilot did not answer. Now I was concerned.

The engineer's voice came through the intercom. "Don't call the pilot again, he's falling apart."

I did not like the tone of his voice. He seemed scared. I kept monitoring the ailing engine from my waist window.

We were approaching our base and with a bit of luck we could land safely. My concern was justified. I saw the first tongues of flames flicker out over the wing from #4 engine.

"The engine is on fire," I warned the pilot. There was no answer.

"I repeat the engine is on fire." There was silence from the cockpit.

I gathered my students on top of the wing internal section where they would be safer in a crash. As we were coming in for a landing, the tower told us to go around again as one main gear was not down and that the engine was on fire.

The pilot pulled the nose of the plane up, but did not hit the engine throttles. The next thing I saw was the ground coming up to meet us.

I had a flashback to the plane that lifted us from the airfield in Yugoslavia and the cliff in front of us, the one that the amazing pilot had lifted the plane over.

The Last Mission

I was praying that this pilot could be as skillful, but that was a hopeless prayer. I braced myself as the plane dove into the stall. The nose hit the ground.

The impact of the crash was tremendous. Bodies were thrown all around. Aircraft parts shot up into the air. "How ironic," I thought. I had survived the thick enemy flak, and a shot down plane, I had survived the Germans and Chetniks, the suffering of hunger, endless walking and terrible living conditions. And I had survived legions of lice, only to end up dead in a crash in a cotton field in Texas during a training mission.

But my lucky streak was still with me.

Not only did I remain alive, but the impact of the crash buried the flaming engine enough in the soft ground to keep the fire contained.

I urged the students to exit through the waist window. Then, I went to the fuselage extinguisher location to get the fire extinguisher. I got out to the wing with the fire extinguisher to put out the last remnants of the engine fire. After the fire was out, I crawled under the badly crushed front of the plane and rushed to help the people trapped in the crumpled front of the fuselage.

The pilot was frozen in his seat. His eyes and mouth were wide open. It was hard to say if he was dead or alive.

The sirens sounded near. Soon the fire wagon, the big wrecker, and the ambulance arrived.

Miraculously, most of the people got out safely with only a few minor cuts and bruises.

A New Life

There were more people trapped under the top of the gun turret, up front.

"Are you okay?" the medic asked me.

It was then that I felt a sharp pain in my back and collapsed. The last thing I remembered was being loaded on a stretcher into the ambulance, and the big wrecker boom trying to lift the top of the gun turret, where some of the crew was trapped.

When I came to in the hospital, I found out that I had suffered rib separation, a fractured back, and a concussion.

I spent several days in the hospital.

As for the pilot, he was later discharged from the service. It was determined, after a hearing, that he was not fit to fly under pressure, and that the crash was listed as "pilot error".

One month later, I was back on flying status. On my first mission after the crash, everything went well except just before the landing. As we approached the runway, the #4 engine suddenly quit. The pilot did everything he possibly could, but the landing was short of the runway.

The plane hit the dirt and then the cement runway, both main landing gear tires blew out, and we ended up dragging the tail down the runway. Luckily, none of the crew was seriously injured.

It was after that incident that the flight surgeon called me to his office. He looked at me and shook his head in disbelief.

"You know, Kollar, it's time for you to be grounded." As much as I loved flying, I knew he was right.

"I know sir, I think the Good Lord is trying to tell me something."

I was assigned to Base Intelligence library where I was to teach gunnery students what to do to handle the situation of being shot down in enemy territory.

Teaching for me was routine. My fascination was with engines and with the dynamics of mechanisms. I could spend endless hours trying to figure out how things worked.

Then something happened that broke the routine. It was a blind date with a girl who worked in the Headquarters of the Intelligence Office. Her name was Polly. At our first meeting, I experienced an unknown sensation. My heart pounded fast against my chest, my legs weakened, and a wave of an uncustomary energy penetrated through out my body.

On our first date, we went out to dinner. As we talked about ourselves, I wanted to tell her about my adventure in Yugoslavia. I wanted so badly to tell her every detail. This was the first time that I wanted to impress someone by bragging about my unbelievable survival.

With great difficulty, I kept the classified information to myself.

After dinner, I dropped Polly off at her place. As I escorted her to the door, I knew I was in love. Standing in front of her door, I said, "Someday I am going to marry

A New Life

you." She looked at me with eyes wide open from her apparent surprise at my statement.

She began to laugh and said, "Oh, Bill, you don't even know me. This is our first date."

The truth is that I surprised myself with my bold approach.

But for the days to come, I was certain that Polly was the girl of my dreams. She was constantly on my mind, and all that mattered was our next date.

Things were going great between Polly and me, until the order came for my transfer to Lockbourne Air Force Base in Ohio.

Our first separation was a new experience for both of us. We were missing each other terribly. After a few months, Polly managed to get a transfer to Lockbourne and all was right with the world.

On May 12, 1945, my prophecy came true. Polly and I were married in Adrian, Michigan.

In November of 1945 I was honorably discharged from the Air Force.

I was still being tormented by the urge to reveal the details of my ordeal on the ground in Yugoslavia to Polly. Eventually, I learned to live with that urge.

Shortly after our wedding day, Polly and I decided to visit my mother in Grand Rapids, Michigan. We had a twenty-five foot glider house trailer and this was our first trip together. After a short visit with my mother, we headed south. We were determined to make this a special trip.

The Last Mission

We loaded the trailer with all the necessities and food and we were even prepared in case the car broke down, by taking a second car.

Polly drove our 1937 Cord car and I pulled the trailer with our Nash convertible. But the one thing we did not count on was the weather. On the first afternoon of our trip, snow began to fall. The visibility was bad and driving became a challenge.

My car began to make rattling sounds and the steering wheel vibrated. Polly led the way. It was impossible for her to see me through the heavy snowstorm. As I was slowing down and she was pulling farther ahead, I blew my horn to catch her attention but she could not hear me. So, she went on driving.

I found a gas station and pulled in. The mechanic found nothing wrong with the car. I rotated the tires, thinking that this was the problem. But, the rattling sound continued.

Finally, I found that a large nut was missing under the car. That nut was holding the backing plate on the front wheel hub. The problem was fixed and I was ready to go. In my eagerness to fix the car, though, I had forgotten Polly. She was nowhere to be found.

Our contact person in case of separation was Aunt Hazel in Pontiac, Illinois.

"She just called and left a number," Aunt Hazel told me over the phone. I called that number and to my relief Polly answered.

"Where are you?" I asked.

When she told me where she was I was shocked. "You are over 200 miles away," I said, trying to stay calm

"Well, it is very hilly in Missouri and I thought that you were right behind me."

I did not know what to say.

"Bill, I'm cold and I've been waiting here for you for a while, already."

"I know, I know, but there is no way to pull the trailer through these road conditions," I said.

"Well, there is another problem." "What now?" I asked

"The Cord will not start."

I knew that it might be days before I could get the trailer through the heavily snowed-in roads.

"Do you think you can hitchhike back here?" I asked Polly.

"I will try, Bill."

Polly had stopped at a gas station. From there, she found two soldiers who had just been discharged from the service to give her a ride back. Meanwhile, the gas station owner was kind enough to push the Cord into a work bay. The '36 Chevy that the two soldiers drove had no heater. About six hours later, they arrived at the gas station where I was. Polly was freezing under a military blanket.

We treated the two soldiers to a T-bone steak dinner in the trailer and then they headed north into the storm.

Polly and I decided to spend the night there.

The weather was not any better in the morning; however, we decided to move on. The snow had covered the earth, heavily. It was impossible to tell where the edges of the road were. The road we drove along was deserted. We drove extremely slowly.

Suddenly, on one of the turns, the trailer wheels fell off the pavement and swung the trailer and jackknifed the car and trailer off the road.

Thank God there was no traffic, and we were traveling at a slow speed. By now, I was really determined to move on despite the obstacles.

Polly sat quietly in her seat. Finally, after many attempts, I managed to turn the car back in the right direction. A few miles down the road, we found a roadside park along the river. We were just outside of Joplin, Missouri. The trailer's homemade generator gave us lights and we used our kerosene heater to keep the trailer warm. We had enough food and water.

The snow was piling up. It kept falling for a couple of days.

The few days parked in the roadside park gave Polly and me a chance to spend time with just us. It was an unforgettable honeymoon in the wilderness.

When the snowplows came to make a few passes on the highway, we were reminded that there was civilization on this earth. We hooked the trailer up to the Nash and took off. We drove to the gas station where Polly had left the Cord. The car started up on the first try.

A New Life

I explained to Polly that the Cord was far ahead in technology. First it had front wheel drive, and it also had an electro vacuum gearshift. The reason that the Cord would not start was that the grease on the vacuum control froze and wouldn't let the starter switch engage.

"Oh, I see," said Polly to be polite. I looked at her and smiled.

I knew Polly was very special. As I spent more time with her it was a confirmation of my choice to spend my life by her side.

We found a trailer park in Fort Worth, Texas, and parked our trailer.

Eventually, we decided to return to the valley of Texas, where Polly and I had met. It was there that we wanted to build our future.

We decided to build a trailer park at Brownsville. While in Brownsville, I found out that Clark Fetterman, was stationed there in Fort Worth. We met for lunch.

When he heard my idea, he wanted to be a partner in the trailer park. I was always fond of Clark. We had been through a lot together.

He was being discharged in few days. After his discharge the three of us headed to Brownsville, Texas, where we found a four-acre plot. We paid $1000 an acre and began to build our trailer park.

Bill and Polly, the early years

A New Life

CHAPTER 26

The Heartbeat of War

The trailer park was to be built on Boca Chica Highway. After a few months of hard work, the trailer park was ready. We moved our trailer in, and used part of it for an office.

Our first customer was a stray dog. After I petted her head and looked into her eyes, we adopted her. We named her Sandy.

Clark bought himself a small trailer and brought his mother from Pennsylvania to live with him.

Among the people who lived in the trailer park was a mechanic named Ken Mohler. Ken and I became good friends and decided to open a garage and body shop next to the trailer park.

Clark's mother grew increasingly unhappy. "I don't like pioneering," she would often say.

Due to an unhappy mother, Clark sold his part of the park to Ken Mohler and headed back to Pennsylvania.

It was at that time that the Americans began to become heavily involved with the Korean War.

Listening to the news reports about the war on the radio brought up a feeling of great nostalgia.

Suddenly, the problems of the trailer park seemed large, the septic system always needed care. I grew tired of listening to people complaining. And none of our businesses were making much money, anyway.

"We are going to sell everything," I told Polly one day.

"And what are you going to do?" she asked. "I am going to re-enlist in the Air Force."

Polly knew that the military was where I belonged. "Whatever you think is best, is okay with me," Polly said

"The only bad thing about re-enlisting is that I'll be away for a while, but in the long run, it will be better for us," I said.

Polly wrapped her arms around my neck. "I love you Bill Kollar," she said kissing me gently.

My new specialty was to teach jet aircraft engine classes. In just a few months, I was promoted to tech sergeant and transferred to the F-84 and F-89 specialist course. The F-89 was a two-jet aircraft, and extremely heavy. Since, jet mechanics were very much in demand in the Korean War, I knew with my specialty I would have a great chance of going to Korea.

In March of 1951, I was selected for reassignment in Korea.

Polly and I said our long good-byes.

"Promise me that you will be careful." It was the last thing that she said.

The train took me to California three days later. From the docks of San Francisco, I boarded a troop ship.

The Last Mission

Our sleeping quarters on the ship were five-high tiers of hammocks. I was glad that I was on the highest tier, because there was a crack in one of the ship's iron plates and it let water into that area. The water sloshed back and forth as the ship rocked and we hung our belongings off of the floor to keep them dry.

The second day out on the open sea, we ran into bad weather. Immense waves tilted the ship to as much as 30° The old vessel creaked under the strong waves. It was a frightening experience·.

Every time a high wave knocked the ship to its side, I held my breath.

There were seasick people everywhere. You could hardly find an open toilet; even the sailors had their heads in the john. The intense rocking of the ship continued for two days.

After surviving the high waves, the seasickness, and the lousy food, we arrived in Japan, nine days later.

Military trucks took us from the port to an airfield.

From there, we flew to Korea.

At the airfield in Korea, a jeep was waiting for me to take me to the 49th field maintenance squadron. I was surprised to see so much snow on the ground. I arrived on the field after hours, and was given an unused hut in the back of the barracks. I was to spend the night here on a cot, with a little stove to keep me warm. I set my cot up next to the stove, but it was impossible to keep warm. The snow outside had piled up over a foot and it was still snowing. I

The Heartbeat of War

had seldom been so cold in my life.

I was glad to move into the barracks the next day.

The work there was long and tiring. Most of the time we worked 14 hours a day, every day of the week, to keep up with the demands of the damaged planes.

The 49th field maintenance squadron was stationed at K2. Its exact location was unknown to us and to our families. The primary planes on our base were the F-84s. The planes flew as many as four missions a day to support the efforts of the ground troops.

After the Yugoslavian experience, I gain enough weight to reach 165 pounds, which was my normal weight.

When I left Korea, after one year later, hard work and terrible food, left 135 pounds on my body.

CHAPTER 27

The Aftermath of Wars

I left Korea with the rank of Master Sergeant.

It had been a year since I'd seen my wife. I was anxious for the moment that I could hold her in my arms again. Our reunion was emotional. She cried and I thought, "Hell, what's that nonsense that men don't cry?" And since a few lakes of tears were forming behind my eyes, I let a couple tears of love roll down my cheeks.

After spending fifteen wonderful days with Polly, I reported back to Bryan Air Force Base in Bryan, Texas. Since Polly was working at Sheppard Air Force Base Hospital, I applied for a transfer there. The transfer was granted and we were together again.

About two years later, in 1955, I re-enlisted for six more years and was transferred to Chanute Air Force Base, in Illinois.

There, I was assigned as a supervisor of the jet engine course, where I had 35 instructors, both civilians and military, and over 900 students.

In 1957, I was re-assigned to Field Training Detachment and sent to New Mexico to teach about the J57 engine. Those were difficult years because Polly and I spent so much time apart. But 1957 was a happy year for us because Polly delivered our only child, a boy, on August 13th.

Later, I was traveling with Polly and our son from New Mexico to Luke Air Force Base in Phoenix, Arizona. But after a few months in Phoenix, I was separated from them once again when I was sent to Taiwan. There, I was to teach Chinese pilots about the F-100 aircraft, which the U.S.A. was sending to them. I was missing my wife and son terribly. Life was boring there. This was more of a diplomatic assignment and we had to attend parties almost every night.

The diplomatic circle was too pretentious for me. Besides my family, I missed flying and I missed engines.

After seven months in Taiwan, I was sent to England to teach, and in 1959 our detachment was sent to Chambly, Franee, to again teach about the F-100 aircraft, until General De Gaulle threw us out by closing several American bases.

The cold war between two giants, the United States and the Soviet Union, now overshadowed the theater of international politics. It was an era when political mythological figures had risen in the pages of history. It was a time when politics crept into people's lives. The two giants scrambled to move into a favorable position, using the earth as their chessboard. New states were forming, new border lines were drawn, old friends had become enemies, and old rivals had made a truce. The world was divided because of increasingly bitter and unyielding views. The Americans and the Russians were the real victors. They were the ones who had made positive gains because of the wars. All the other victorious states had simply won their survival.

The Soviet Union had greater military strength than ever.

The root of the American empire lay in economic strength.

America became a great creditor to the world, a world that needed so much that no one else could supply.

The Russian Red Army overpowered and occupied every land they desired. The war-torn states, and their exhausted armies, could not stand up to the red war machine.

While the American political system was running methodically and building the new technology of military supremacy, the rest of the world was staggering under the troubles of recovery. Over fifteen million Europeans were killed during the Great War, and those who survived lived amidst the ruins. The European currencies had totally collapsed, factories were destroyed, and communication centers were shattered.

The civilized society of Europe had given way to the horror of Nazi warfare. In the name of survival, swindling and cheating were transformed into acts of virtue. The struggle against German occupying forces had created new divisions. The firing squads went to work settling old scores. Dictatorships and civil wars flourished in almost every country.

The once powerful European industrial machine was now silent. Transportation was ruined as bridges, roads, and railroad tracks were destroyed. Dictatorships and civil

The Aftermath of Wars

wars were not isolated only to Europe. It was a global phenomenon.

In many cases, the great social and economic problems were not addressed by the superpowers because of unavailability of manpower or the unavailability of funding, as well as the fear of risking their relationships with certain countries. The imbalance and injustice of the social distribution became a burden on the world's conscience. Many who viewed this as a great injustice, used it as a powerful weapon for nationalistic revolutions.

Vicious guerrilla wars and fanatical terrorism have claimed thousands of lives since. The majority of lives lost were innocent bystanders. In the post war years, a tremendous human suffering occurred around the world. But one thing is certain: nothing inhumane, nothing abusive, will ever defeat the human spirit.

The spirit called, freedom.

CHAPTER 28

A Full Circle

*I*t was amazing how a generic letter on an inert piece of paper had activated memories and aroused emotions nested in the deep chambers of my memory. Long ago, I had made a promise not to reveal the details that led to our survival. I kept my promise! I did not reveal the details even to the person I love the most, the person who has become the other part of myself.

Polly looked at me with admiration.

"Oh, Bill, the things that you went through," she said. I bowed my head. I was never comfortable receiving praise.

"Well, I hope that it was worth it, that we were able to make a difference for the younger generation."

I believe, that during the moments of warfare, a seed was planted in my mind, a seed that changed the meaning of my life.

As my mind ranged over the history of the Great War, it was clear to me that the war, that any war, was not restricted to a conflict between countries. It was the eternal struggle between good and evil. The images of torture, the inhumane massacres, hammered constantly in my mind.

A Full Circle

The very idea that I was part of the Great War added an immeasurable force behind my struggle for freedom. It was this force that has made my existence in this world bearable.

Now that I have lived in the pages of history books and stood beside heroes with indomitable spirit, I feel courage rising in my soul. Courage that blossomed from the seed of freedom.

Now, in the twilight of my life, I felt compelled to tell my story. I must leave behind my desires, my experience and my message. The military service is never forgotten by anyone who experiences it. Old people speak of it with unconcealed nostalgia, with the wistfulness one has for a good experience. In some cases, the memory bares the nightmare of bullying and cruelty.

The military is a mixture that contains a number of elements. The military offered the opportunity for a young man to experience rare feelings. I felt great satisfaction on my graduation day as an airplane mechanic. I had proud moments, one of which was while marching in formation past Old Glory, my first day in school.

I lived fascinating times in school where I left not an inch of the airplane unexamined.

The trails in the air depot in Albuquerque, where there were no warplanes but twenty-mile hikes with full packs and gas masks.

Unforgettable faces that I remember with reverence. One of them is my first instructor and good friend

Mark Ebert who was adored and emulated by all. There were thrilling moments, like my first airplane ride in a T-6 at the gunnery school in Laredo, Texas, when I sat in the rear cockpit facing backwards, and I saw the ground drop away from the plane during takeoff. This was my first airplane ride, ever.

And it was destiny on Biggs Field, Texas, where I met the Maggie's Drawers crew, the one that I was to share an unbelievable adventure with. Together, after our advance training in Tucson, Arizona, we boarded a ship to Casablanca, a ship that on its way back was torpedoed and destroyed by the Germans.

In Casablanca, we stayed in an infantry tent city. That was the first time that I experienced unbelievable human tragedy. It was a scene that broke my heart. There were endless casualties, ruins everywhere; the whole population had turned into beggars. Running sores, bad diseases, deformities, people without arms or without legs were everywhere I looked. It brought tears to my eyes.

The food in our camp was inedible; time and time again the entire camp was under a roaring siege of diarrhea. Daytime was burning hot and nighttime was freezing cold. We left the devastated people behind and were flown to Manduria, Italy. The picture of suffering, the smell of death, remained intact in my mind.

From Manduria we found our way to Lecce, Italy. Now, my story has been told, at last.

I am content with the thought that my life has come

A Full Circle

full circle. I have a good life, and I am blessed with freedom and love.

The sun was setting in the west, the sky golden and bright. Soon, another day would surrender its existence into the pitiless embrace of unforgiving time. I held Polly's hand. Next to her, time had reached infinity. We looked at each other and smiled. I was convinced that after all that I had lived and loved, she had become my rock.

Ours is a love that surpassed all other feelings and emotions.

Bill and Clarence in downtown Casablanca

My first instructor, Mark Ebert, was killed in a bombing mission on April 4th, 1944, two days after I was shot down in my last mission.

My older brother, Harold, died at 75 years old of Parkinson's Disease.

Fred Stryker, our pilot, was captured by the Germans. Both of his legs were amputated. He remained a POW until the end of the war.

EPILOGUE

Eternal Dilemma

You know the story.

The story of wars and the eternal struggle for an illusion called victory.

The story about wars made up of myths of the eternal heroes and the classic villains.

War is a subject that the writer must explore in all of its aspects, its possibilities, and its consequences.

As a writer, I must examine and understand why wars have transformed glory and legend into tragedy and chaos.

War opens up a box full of enigmas, a labyrinth of mixed feelings and unpredictable reactions.

The danger that always exists is a story that repeats itself, a story that remains unexamined.

Every war seems all new, but in reality it is the same war, all over again.

It is a concept that repeats the means in a way that seems as though it is being done for the first time.

Countless writers use World War II as a prototype to chronicle other wars.

World War II was an event full of ideologies and

feelings, a war that covered reality and fantasy without separating them.

It was a time that the whole population of this planet was affected.

A war with deep roots of hate. Nazism is based on hate,

A poisonous feeling that motivated the gangsters of Germany, Italy and Japan to conspire in an attempt to destroy the world.

The means of World War II was one and the same as that which created barbaric conflicts in the pre-civilized era, aggression!

With aggression, human feelings are muted and priority is given to resentment.

It is a time that people become enemies and feel nothing for one another.

Wars do that.

Wars drain away all that makes one human.

Even we who did not witness the death camps, the killing of children, the torture and rape,

Even we are still mentally brutalized by the images of unbelievable human suffering.

Because of that, we have lost a part of our being.

When the fighting finally ended, there was a chasm between those who read about the war and those who witnessed the brutalities, a chasm that never closed.

It is true that the writer cries and laughs between the lines of the written word,

That he hurts, dies and suffers among the pages of the written story.

The writer relives the events in a way that affects every dimension of his existence.

But, it is impossible to enter the realm of the spirit of those who physically experienced the fear of death, the exultation of victory.

It is impossible to capture the dreams they dreamed and the nightmares they awoke with.

In the realm of logic, we who never witnessed their suffering will be forever strangers to those who were brutalized.

Brutalization, rape, torture, and any other severe suffering, are kinds of pain that remain concealed within the compounds of shame,

A feeling that rarely is shared with others.

The writer is left with the task to uncover the pain that wars have created.

This writer does not want to see a repetition of World War II, a realization that came after seeing the civilian population waking up from the sleep of aggression and nothingness, to finally see the truth of the terrible results of warfare,

Today, in the aftermath of countless narratives of this eternal story called World War II, we can understand what happened in the trenches.

Now it is time to leave the recounting of wars to the historians who so brilliantly illustrate them.

It is time to discover the human effect that war has created.

An attempt to close the chasm of pain will be the biggest honor we can offer to the heroes who fought in the wars.

The time has come to examine the consequences of war, to stop the cannons ready to flare up their fire, a fire that has already consumed tens of millions of men, women, and children all over the world.

I am hopeful that we can honor their sacrifice by yearning for personal freedom and peace among nations.

We must not abandon our dream of dreams, To finally see peace among all people on earth.

— Nikos Ligidakis

About the author

Award winning author, Nikos Ligidakis, writes with clarity and passion in an ardent voice, not to just recount adventures, but with an expression of feelings, to encourage the reader to think, to find hope in the eternal struggle for the meaning of life and the awareness of harmony. Nikos is the author of several historical fiction and biography books.

"As a writer, my aspiration has always been to share my perspective on what it means to be a human being, in all its complexities. I wanted to tell a story that reflects a comparative importance of political structures, religions and histories of the past. My books represent a lifelong dream of putting into narrative form, my many observations of the brilliance and kindness of the human spirit: people at their worst and people at their best. It is my intention to engage the reader in the process of observing history in both times past and in current day happenings for the sole purpose of gaining greater clarity in the shaping of one's own approach to life and the deepening of individual insight."

— *Nikos Ligidakis*

www.ingramcontent.com/pod-product-compliance
Lightning Source LLC
Chambersburg PA
CBHW030530100426
42813CB00001B/204